Children's Stories from the *Dawn-Breakers*

This book belongs to

____

Children's Stories from the *Dawn-Breakers*

written by Zoe Meyer
illustrated by Winifred Barnum-Newman

BELLWOOD PRESS®
EVANSTON, ILLINOIS

Bellwood Press, 1233 Central Street, Evanston, Illinois 60202

 Published 2000
Printed in the United States of America
29 28 27 26 4 3 2

Library of Congress Cataloging-in-Publication Data

Myer, Zoe.
Children's stories from The dawn-breakers / by Zoe Meyer ; with illustrations by Winifred Barnum-Newman.
p. cm.
"Based on Nabil-i-A'zam's [sic] The dawn-breakers."—P.
Summary: Explore the history and teachings of the Bahai Faith and some of the important figures in this religion's development.
ISBN 0-87743-035-7 (softcover)
1. Bahai Faith—Juvenile literature. 2. Babism—Juvenile literature. 3. Bab, 'Ali Muḥammad Shirazi, 1819–1850—Juvenile literature. 4. Bahá'u'lláh, 1817–1892—Juvenile literature. [1. Bahai Faith. 2. Babism. 3. Bab, 'Ali Muḥammad Shirazi, 1819–1850. 4. Baháu'lláh, 1817–1892.] I. Newman, Winifed Barnum, ill. II. Nabil Zrandi, 1831–1892. Tarikh-i Nabil. III. Title.
BP330.N313 1998
297.9'3'09–DC21 98-3403
CIP
AC

Contents

List of Illustrations ix

1 Shaykh Aḥmad's Secret 1

2 The Young Man in the Green Turban 5

3 The Shepherd's Dream 11

4 Mullá Ḥusayn and the Báb 15

5 The Letters of the Living 21

6 The Story of the Báb 25

7 The Báb's Messengers 31

8 The Message to Bahá'u'lláh 37

9 The Dream of Bahá'u'lláh's Father 41

10 The Storm 47

11 The Story of Mullá Ṣádiq 53

12 The Báb Is Taken Prisoner 57

13 The White Bird 61

14 The Plague 65

15 On the Road to Ṭihrán 69

16 The Castle of Máh-Kú 73

17 ‘Alí Khán’s Dream 79

18 Ṭáhirih 83

19 The New Order 87

20 Muḥammad-‘Alí’s Vision 93

21 The Trial of the Báb 97

22 Fort Ṭabarsí 101

23 The Siege 105

24 The Death of Quddús 111

25 The Story of Vaḥíd 115

26 The Martyrdom of the Báb 119

27 Ḥujjat 127

28 Bahá'u'lláh 133

29 God's Cause Today 139

Glossary of Symbols 145

List of Illustrations

Shaykh Aḥmad 1

"Let us imagine we are going with Shaykh Aḥmad on this journey. We would have to walk much of the way, or ride a horse or donkey." 3

Siyyid Káẓim and his friend 6

"He gave them a drink from a beautiful silver cup." 9

"He had been watching his sheep in a pasture nearby when he fell asleep and began to dream." 12

"Mullá Ḥusayn went to a place where he could be quiet and pray." 15

"As Mullá Ḥusayn left the Báb he was so excited and so happy that he trembled and could hardly walk. People who saw him must have wondered what had happened, but you can be sure he kept his great Secret." 18

"'Alí seemed to see a light that moved ahead of him." 20

"The sun sends its light and heat to the earth to make the trees and flowers and everything grow." 28

"The man prostrated himself and began to pray." 34

"A great number of fishes came." 43

"A terrible storm came up. The big waves must have looked like mountains to the people in the small ship." 46

"For days they had to satisfy their thirst with the juice of lemons instead of water." 48

"A man who lived in the desert . . . crept up softly, snatched the Báb's saddlebag, which was lying on the ground near Him, and ran away with it." 50

"All of the time while he was being whipped and blood was running from his wounds, Mullá Ṣádiq was calm and smiling and seemed not even to be feeling it." 54

"The governor . . . sent out a company of soldiers on horseback to find the Báb and bring Him back in chains." 58

"He seemed to see a man talking to a great number of people." 61

"One night 'Abdu'l-Karím had another vision. He saw before him a bird, white as snow, hovering above his head." 63

"They found people running this way and that, as if they were trying to get away from something. . . . Then they saw a long train of coffins being hurried through the street, each followed by men and women shrieking and wailing." 66

"The constable did as the Báb had said, and at once the son became well." 68

"They camped on a beautiful hill with orchards and meadows all about." 71

"The Castle of Máh-Kú was high up on a mountain in a very lonely part of the country." 74

"He wrote a very great book that became the Law for His day." 77

"'Alí Khán walked toward the river, and as he reached the bridge he saw two men coming toward him, one walking before the other." 80

"Her name was Ṭáhirih." 83

"They followed a lonely road until they came to Ṭihrán at dawn." 85

"Ṭáhirih herself came in. And to everyone's great astonishment, she was not wearing a veil." 90

"Even the animals seemed to love the Báb, for if they had been fierce, they became gentle in His presence." 97

"Quddús arrived at the fort during the night. . . . Mullá Ḥusayn and one hundred men went to meet him. Each man carried two lighted candles." 100

"Mullá Ḥusayn's horse became entangled in a tent rope, and before it could get away, a bullet struck Mullá Ḥusayn in the chest." 108

"Quddús wore the green turban that the Báb had sent to him and rode the horse sent by the prince who was at the head of the enemy's army." 112

"Every time they rushed forth with their cry of 'Alláh-u-Akbar' they frightened the enemy and scattered them." 115

"'Send me not from Thee, O Master,' he begged. 'Wherever Thou goest, suffer me to follow Thee.'" 121

"The evil command was carried out. The Báb and Muḥammad-'Alí were both killed." 125

"At last one day Zaynab had her wish, for she was shot while helping to drive back the enemy." 130

"Whenever 'Abdu'l-Bahá was sent out on the street, other boys of His age would run after Him, pelting Him with stones." 135

"He was treated with the greatest cruelty and was imprisoned in a dark underground dungeon." 136

Shaykh Aḥmad's Secret

Many years ago there lived in Persia a man who knew a very wonderful secret. Perhaps you would not think it a secret, because it was written in a Book so that everyone might read it. But those who read it did not understand just what it meant. Shaykh Aḥmad understood because he had studied this Book a great deal and had prayed to understand. And the secret he found there made him so happy that he wished to tell everyone.

Would you like to know the secret? In this Book, which was called the Qur'án, it said that God would send a new Teacher to the world, a very great Teacher like Jesus and Muḥammad.

We know only a little about God because He is so much greater than we are, and so very wonderful. Sometimes we become so busy living our lives from day to day that we forget about God. We forget that we would not even be alive if He had not given us life. So once in a while He sends one of these divine Teachers to the world to remind people about Himself. These Teachers are like Him, and They show us how He wishes us to live.

Jesus was one of these Teachers. Many people know about Him and read about Him in the Bible. Others know about Muḥammad and read about Him in the Qur'án. It was in the Qur'án, which Muḥammad revealed long ago, that Shaykh Aḥmad read about the new Teacher Who was coming. He was called the Promised One because God had promised He would come.

Other people read about the Promised One in the Qur'án and knew He was to come. But here is the difference between them and Shaykh Aḥmad: When Shaykh Aḥmad read the words, he felt very sure that it was time for the Promised One to come right away. The others thought that He would not come for a long, long time.

Shaykh Aḥmad felt as he read the words that the Promised One was living on the earth at that very time. He knew that he must go out and find Him and tell others about Him. Surely everyone would wish to know.

To do this he had to leave his home and his family and travel all over the country. In those days there were no telephones or radios or newspapers. There were not even trains to carry mail. And of course there were no airplanes. So, if anyone had something he wished people to know, he had to go to them.

Let us imagine we are going with Shaykh Aḥmad on this journey. We would have to walk much of the way, or ride a horse or donkey. And at night we could not go to a comfortable hotel for food and rest, because there were no hotels such as we have now. At that time they were called "caravansaries," and we would not find them very comfortable.

But Shaykh Aḥmad did not mind being uncomfortable, because he knew he was doing what God wished him to do. And he was so happy that people wanted to know what he knew. Wherever he went they came in great numbers to hear him talk about the Promised One

Who was to come. Shaykh Aḥmad would read to them from the Qur'án because many of them did not know how to read. You see, they did not have schools such as we have. After he had read, he would talk about the Promised One and about how they would know Him when He came.

News about Shaykh Aḥmad traveled all over the country, and the Sháh, who was the ruler of the country, invited him to come for a visit. This made people jealous, and they urged their friends and relatives not to listen to Shaykh Aḥmad. Sometimes they tried to quarrel with him and have him put out of their cities.

Did this keep Shaykh Aḥmad from telling his great News? Not for one moment! Many people believed him and followed him wherever he went so that they might hear more about the Promised One. They knew that He would be a very wonderful person. They knew He would love everyone. He would be kind and would help all who needed Him. How they must have longed to find Him.

After many years of traveling in this way, Shaykh Aḥmad knew that he had finished what God wished him to do. Others must now carry on the work he had begun. So he called Siyyid Káẓim, his very dear friend, to him. He asked him to travel in his place and tell the people about the Promised One.

Siyyid Káẓim promised to do this for, like Shaykh Aḥmad, he wanted everyone to hear this wonderful News. And perhaps someday he might see the Promised One for himself.

The Young Man in the Green Turban

Do you remember the story of Shaykh Aḥmad, who traveled about, telling the people that God was sending a new Teacher? When Shaykh Aḥmad died, he left Siyyid Káẓim to carry on his work and spread the news of the Promised One.

Perhaps the word "Siyyid" is unfamiliar. It means a member of the family of Muḥammad, the great Teacher Who revealed the Qur'án. Of course, Muḥammad had lived many years before that, but all of the men who were later born in that family were called Siyyids. It was a great honor to be related to Muḥammad, even if it was many, many years later.

Here is another thing Siyyid Káẓim told the people: This divine Teacher Whom God had promised was living at that very time. Perhaps He was even living nearby and they did not know Him. You can imagine how surprised the people were to hear this, how they must have talked about it and wondered who the Promised One was and where He lived. If you and I had been there, we probably would have wondered, too.

It is strange, but when God sends a new divine Teacher to the earth to remind people of Him, only a few recognize Him at first. They may see Him on the street or in the shrine where He goes to pray and yet not know Him, because their hearts are not full of love and hope. And some people do not recognize Him because they are so busy thinking about themselves.

There are many others, however, who are not like these people. Their hearts are ready because they are expecting Him. Siyyid Káẓim was one of these. And he was trying to prepare others to recognize the Promised One when they saw Him. This story tells about a very happy day in Siyyid Káẓim's life, the day he first met the Promised One. And he not only met Him but he heard Him talk.

Now I must tell you something that even Siyyid Káẓim, perhaps, did not know at that time. God really sent two divine Teachers instead of one. The One of Whom Siyyid Káẓim was telling them was called the Báb. The word "Báb" means "gate" or "door," and it was just as if the Báb came to open the door for Bahá'u'lláh, the other great Teacher, Who came later. The Báb, of course, came first. He was the One Whom Shaykh Aḥmad and Siyyid Káẓim were expecting because they had read about Him in the Qur'án.

One morning very, very early, just at dawn, Siyyid Káẓim sent a messenger to a friend, telling him that a very important person had arrived in Karbilá, where they were living, and that they must visit him at once. When the friend arrived at

Siyyid Káẓim's house, he found Siyyid Káẓim dressed and waiting at the door. They walked through the streets together.

How quiet it must have been in the city, for the sun was not yet up, and the people had not begun to stir about. They soon reached a house where a Young Man stood in the doorway, as if waiting for them. He wore a green turban, and His face was so gentle and kind that it seemed no one who saw Him could help loving Him. Have you seen people you loved the first time you met them?

Coming to meet the two friends, the Young Man put His arms around Siyyid Káẓim and spoke to him such words of loving-kindness that Siyyid Káẓim could only stand with bowed head. He could not speak.

The Young Man led Siyyid Káẓim and his friend into the house and upstairs to a room decorated with flowers, which gave out a very lovely perfume. Here He told them to be seated, and He gave them a drink from a beautiful silver cup that stood in the center of the room.

When you love someone very, very much, you feel so happy that you just want to be near them. You do not need to talk. That is the way the two visitors felt that morning while they were with the Young Man. Only a few words were spoken. Then He led them to the door and, with a wonderful smile, told them good-bye.

How often the friend who had gone with Siyyid Káẓim must have thought of this visit. Then, three days later, Siyyid Káẓim saw this Young Man again. Siyyid

Káẓim was teaching a number of people about the Qur'án when the Young Man entered and sat down with them. At once Siyyid Káẓim stopped speaking. When the others asked him to continue, he only shook his head. He pointed to a ray of sunlight that came in at the door and fell upon the lap of the Young Man.

"What more shall I say?" Siyyid Káẓim replied, turning his face toward the Young Man. "The Truth," he said, "is more manifest than the ray of light that has fallen upon that lap!" You see, Siyyid Káẓim knew Who this Young Man was, and he could not understand why the others did not.

But still the others did not understand, not even the one who had gone with Siyyid Káẓim early that other morning. In his heart he had a strange feeling whenever he thought about the Young Man. Several times he had started to ask Siyyid Káẓim the Young Man's name, but something always seemed to stop him.

Perhaps you have guessed Who the Young Man was, but the friend of Siyyid Káẓim did not know, even though he had come to love Him with all his heart and to think of Him many times a day. One day he heard about a Young Man Who said that He was the Báb, the Promised One. Then he knew that this was the One Whom he had seen in Karbilá and had loved so much.

The Shepherd's Dream

Siyyid Káẓim was very happy. He not only knew that the Promised One had come; He had seen Him and visited Him. What a joy it must have been to tell others about Him, even though he was not yet allowed to tell them His name.

But would you believe it? He found many who would not listen. It does no good to try to tell something to someone who does not wish to hear it. Not only did some of the people not listen, sometimes they were very cruel to Siyyid Káẓim and his friends.

Siyyid Káẓim and a few who were his close friends went on teaching just the same, for there were always people who were glad to listen. He read to them from the Qur'án the words which told that there would be two great Teachers. The One they were expecting would come first, but there would be another great Teacher soon after. And this second Teacher would bring His Light to the whole world, not just to the country in which He lived.

One day at noon Siyyid Káẓim was standing in the shade of a palm tree, waiting for the people to come from the noonday prayer. Suddenly an Arabic man rushed up and threw his arms around Siyyid Káẓim.

Here is the strange story the man told him:

Three days before, he had been watching his sheep in a pasture nearby when he fell asleep and began to dream. The man, who was a follower of Muḥammad, dreamed that Muḥammad came to him and told him to listen well and remember

what he was told, for these words were sent from God. "If you be faithful to them," He said, "great will be your reward. If you neglect them, grievous retribution will befall you." Great trouble would come if he forgot the message. Then He told the shepherd to stay near that place. In three days Siyyid Káẓim and his friends would come there at noon to pray. The shepherd was to greet Siyyid Káẓim and to tell him that his work was almost done—that three days after he returned to Karbilá, he would be permitted to go to the One Who was speaking. Soon after that the Promised One would make Himself known to everyone.

Now this dream meant that three days after Siyyid Káẓim returned to his home in Karbilá he would die because his work was finished. Each of us has work to do. If we did not, we would not be here on earth.

The shepherd's words made Siyyid Káẓim very, very happy, but of course they made his friends sad. When Siyyid Káẓim saw this, he said to them, "Is not your love for me for the sake of that true One whose advent we all await? Would you not wish me to die, that the Promised One may be revealed?"

He talked so lovingly to them and it made them so happy to think that at last they should know the Promised One that they ceased to feel sad. And that is the way it is with us today. We never like to lose a friend, but when we do, God always sends us another one.

So Siyyid Káẓim finished his work and returned to Karbilá. There, three days later, as the shepherd had dreamed, Siyyid Káẓim died, leaving his friends to find the Promised One and tell people about Him.

Mullá Ḥusayn and the Báb

After the death of Siyyid Káẓim, it seemed as if his friends did not know what to do. At this time a young man named Mullá Ḥusayn came back to Karbilá. Mullá Ḥusayn was a friend of Siyyid Káẓim who had gone to another city to carry a message for him. At once Mullá Ḥusayn called some of the friends together and asked them what Siyyid Káẓim had said to them before he died.

One of them said he had told them to leave their homes and scatter far and wide to find the Promised One. Another said he had told them the Promised One would guide whoever tried to find Him.

Mullá Ḥusayn begged them to wait no longer. "Why have you chosen to tarry in Karbilá?" he asked. "Your first obligation, as well as mine, is to arise and carry out, both in the spirit and in the letter, the dying message of our beloved chief."

But they all began to make excuses. You know how it is when we do not wish to do something. We can always find an excuse, but the true reason is that we do not wish to do it. At last Mullá Ḥusayn saw that they did not want to go. Feeling very sad, he turned away from them and started out with only his brother and his nephew for companions.

First he felt that he should make himself ready to meet the Promised One. When you are going to meet someone you love, you like to look as good as you can. That is the way Mullá Ḥusayn felt. But he was not thinking of his clothes. He wanted to be ready by making his thoughts right, by thinking as the beloved Promised One would wish him to think, and by doing what He would wish him to do.

So Mullá Ḥusayn went to a place where he could be quiet and pray. He and his companions stayed there for forty days.

At the close of the forty days they started out again to find the Promised One. They stopped at a city nearby and there they had a beautiful experience. The Báb had lived in that city several years before. He had spent much time praying, and these prayers had made the city so different from other cities that, when Mullá Ḥusayn came to it, he could feel the difference. That shows what prayer can do. The Báb had left the city by that time, so Mullá Ḥusayn and his companions did not stay there. They went on to another city named <u>Sh</u>íráz.

When they reached the edge of the city, Mullá Ḥusayn told his brother and his nephew to go ahead and find rooms for them. He would meet them later, when it was time for the evening prayer.

As Mullá Ḥusayn was walking near the edge of the city, a Young Man came up to him. The Young Man wore a green turban and His face was shining with joy, just as your face does when you are very happy.

Mullá Ḥusayn did not know that this Young Man was the Báb, the Promised One for Whom he had been searching. He thought He must be a friend of Siyyid Káẓim who had heard about him and had come to meet him. The Young Man put His arms around Mullá Ḥusayn as if He had known him always. He invited Mullá Ḥusayn to come to His home and rest. But Mullá Ḥusayn told the Young Man that his friends would be expecting him.

"Commit them to the care of God," answered the Young Man. "He will surely protect and watch over them."

He was so gentle and so loving that Mullá Ḥusayn must have been happier than he had ever been in his life. The Báb took him to a small house, where He knocked on the door. An Ethiopian servant let them in, and the Báb Himself brought water and poured it for His visitor to wash his hands. Then they prayed together, and in his prayer Mullá Ḥusayn again asked God to help him find the Promised One. He still did not know that this Young Man was the Promised One.

While they talked, something happened that makes all of us, even now and in years to come, remember that day so many years ago. It was about two hours after sunset when the Báb, with great love and joy, told Mullá Ḥusayn Who He was. Mullá Ḥusayn was so astonished that at first he could not believe the good news. But as the Báb went on talking, Mullá Ḥusayn knew that no one else could be so wise. He knew that this must be the Báb. And the time passed so quickly that they talked all night, but Mullá Ḥusayn did not realize it until he heard the call to prayer in the morning.

"This night," the Báb said, "this very hour, will, in the days to come, be celebrated as one of the greatest and most significant of all festivals."

It was the very first time that the Báb had told anyone Who He was. Wouldn't it be wonderful to be the one He told? Before Mullá Ḥusayn left, the Báb told him that he was the first to believe in Him. Later eighteen souls would find the Báb, just as Mullá

Ḥusayn had done. But Mullá Ḥusayn was to tell no one about the Báb, for each person had to find Him without any help. When all eighteen had learned the great Secret, the Báb would send them out to tell the whole world that a new Teacher had come.

As Mullá Ḥusayn left the Báb he was so excited and so happy that he trembled and could hardly walk. People who saw him must have wondered what had happened, but you can be sure he kept his great Secret.

The Letters of the Living

Mullá Ḥusayn visited the Báb many times. He always went at night so that no one would see him, because each of the first eighteen others to recognize the Báb must find Him for himself. Each day Mullá Ḥusayn could hardly wait for night to come so that he could be with the Báb.

Whenever God sends a new divine Teacher to the earth, this Promised One chooses some of the people who love Him and believe in Him to help Him in His work. Sometimes they are called disciples. When Jesus lived on the earth, He had twelve disciples. When the Báb came, He had more than twelve. You will soon hear how many there were and what He called them.

One night the Báb said to Mullá Ḥusayn, "Tomorrow thirteen of your companions will arrive. To each of them extend the utmost loving-kindness." He told Mullá Ḥusayn to pray that God would lead these men, also, to know the Promised One.

The very next morning thirteen friends of Mullá Ḥusayn arrived in the city. One who was named 'Alí noticed that Mullá Ḥusayn was very happy and that he no longer seemed to be searching for the Promised One. 'Alí asked him why this was. Had he found the Promised One?

‘Alí knew at once that Mullá Ḥusayn had indeed found Him. He begged to be shown the way to the Promised One, but Mullá Ḥusayn shook his head.

“Beseech me not,” he said, “to grant you this favor. Let your trust be in Him for He will surely guide your steps, and appease the tumult of your heart.”

‘Alí told the other friends about this, and all of them prayed that God might lead them to the Promised One.

Three nights after this, while ‘Alí was praying, he had a vision. A vision is something like a dream, except that the person who has it may not be asleep. In his vision ‘Alí seemed to see a light that moved ahead of him. He saw himself following the light and finding the Promised One.

It was night, but ‘Alí rose at once and went to the home of Mullá Ḥusayn. Throwing his arms around his friend, he told him of his vision.

Mullá Ḥusayn was very joyous. “Praise be to God who hath guided us hither!” he said.

When morning came, he took ‘Alí to the home of the Báb. In the door stood the Ethiopian servant, who said that, before daybreak, his Master had called him and told him to open the door and stand ready. “Two guests are to arrive early this morning,” the servant had been told. “Extend to them in My name a warm welcome. Say to them from Me: ‘Enter in the Name of God.’”

As the three talked together that morning, the whole room seemed filled with light. They felt that a new and beautiful Day had come.

Each of 'Alí's twelve companions eventually found the Báb. Some dreamed about Him. Some had a vision of Him while they were praying, and others while they were thinking of Him. And so it went until seventeen people had found Him and become His disciples. They were ready to go out and tell about the New Day. The Báb called them "Letters of the Living." One was a woman. You will hear about her later, in another story.

One night the Báb said to Mullá Ḥusayn, "Tomorrow night the remaining Letter will arrive and will complete the number of My chosen disciples."

The Báb knew ahead of time exactly what was going to happen.

The next evening as the Báb, followed by Mullá Ḥusayn, was going home, a young man, tired and dusty from traveling, rushed up and threw his arms around Mullá Ḥusayn. Looking at the Báb, he said, "Why seek you to hide Him from me? I can recognize Him by His gait."

He knew the Báb just by His walk. Mullá Ḥusayn asked him to wait for a moment. Then he hurried to the Báb and told Him about the traveler.

"Marvel not at his strange behavior," the Báb said. "We know him already. We indeed awaited his coming. Go to him and summon him forthwith to Our presence."

So the dusty young man was led to the Báb, Who greeted him with great joy. The name of this young man was Quddús. And now there were eighteen Letters of the Living, ready to go out and tell of the coming of the Promised One.

The Story of the Báb

Although the Báb was the Promised One Whom God sent to tell people about the New Day, He came to the earth as a little baby, just as all of us must come. No one knew that He was the Promised One until He was twenty-five years old.

When the Báb was very young His father died, and He went to live with His uncle. In Persia in those days, there were no schools such as you go to now, and no books to study except the Qur'án. His uncle put Him in the care of a man who taught from the Qur'án. From the first the Báb learned so quickly that His teacher could not understand it.

One day the teacher asked the Báb to recite the first lines of the Qur'án, but the Boy said He could not recite them unless He knew what they meant. Wishing to see what He would do, the teacher pretended not to know what they meant.

"I know what these words signify," the Boy said. "By your leave, I will explain them."

He explained them in such a wise way and so clearly that His teacher was astonished. He knew then that the Báb did not need a teacher.

The next day the teacher took the Boy to His uncle's office. "I have brought Him back to you," he said. "He is not to be treated as a mere child, for in Him I can already discern evidences of that mysterious power which the Revelation of the Lord of the Age alone can reveal."

The Boy's uncle, however, did not wish Him to stop studying. He looked sternly at the Báb. He told Him that He must do as the other children did—sit quietly and listen carefully to every word spoken by His teacher.

The Báb promised to do this and returned to His school. But He could not be like the other children. His soul knew all things without being taught. Finally His uncle took Him out of school and let Him help him in his business.

Some years after this, when the Báb was old enough, He was married to Khadíjih-Bagum, and a little boy was born to them. He was named Aḥmad, and you can imagine how the father and mother loved him. But one day, while Aḥmad was still very little, he was taken sick and died. Of course the Báb and Khadíjih-Bagum missed him a very great deal, but in spite of this the Báb could not feel sad. He knew that God had a place for His small son. And He prayed that someday He, too, might die in such a way that it would show His love for God. And God answered His prayer. In another story you will hear how the Báb died.

In Persia where the Báb lived, the summer is very, very hot. This did not keep Him from praying many hours a day from the house top. Houses in Persia were built in those days with flat roofs, where people could sit in the evening when it was cool. But the Báb would not wait for evening.

Every Friday at dawn He would go up to the roof and pray until the sun rose. At noon, when the sun was hottest, He would go up to pray again, and He would

be so deep in His prayer that He did not seem to feel the burning rays. Here He would stay until late afternoon, thinking and praying with a heart full of love and joy.

Some thought that He was praying to the sun, but of course this was not true. To Him the sun was a sign of God. The sun sends its light and heat to the earth to make the trees and flowers and everything grow. In the same way, God sends His love to us to help us grow more loving in spirit and more like Him. We could not live without His love any more than the flowers and birds could live without the sun.

The Báb was very gentle and kind to everyone He met. He never seemed to want anything for Himself and always gave the best of everything to others. It made people perfectly happy just to be near Him, and it was the greatest joy in the world to hear Him speak. He was very honest and careful of things belonging to others. Here is a story people tell about Him.

One day while the Báb was in business, a man gave Him something to sell for him. The man told Him just what the price was to be. When the Báb sent him the money for the article, there was more than the man had asked for. So the man wrote to Him to find out why.

The Báb wrote back: "What I have sent you is entirely your due. There is not a single farthing in excess of what is your right. There was a time when the trust you had delivered to Me had attained this value. Failing to sell it at that price, I now feel it My duty to offer you the whole of that sum."

You see, when the Báb did sell the article, it did not bring as much money as it would have a bit earlier. The Báb felt that was His fault because He did not sell it in time. So He sent the man the extra money in addition to what He had received for the article. Not everyone would do that.

It is no wonder that everyone loved the Báb. He never could bear to be unkind to anyone.

The Báb's Messengers

Do you remember the story of how the eighteen Letters of the Living found the Báb?

The Báb thought it was now time for them to scatter all over the land and tell people that the Promised One had come. So one day He called them together to talk to them.

Mullá Ḥusayn was the first to be called to Him. And because the Báb loved Mullá Ḥusayn so much, He told him just a tiny bit about something very wonderful that was going to happen to Mullá Ḥusayn later. He was to go to many cities to give the Báb's message. Then he was to go to the great city of Ṭihrán.

"A secret lies hidden in that city," the Báb said. "When made manifest, it shall turn the earth into paradise."

You see, the Báb did not tell Mullá Ḥusayn what he would find in Ṭihrán. But Mullá Ḥusayn knew it would be something very beautiful that would turn the earth into paradise—that would make it like heaven. Later you will hear about this great secret.

It must have been wonderful to hear what the Báb said to the Letters of the Living when He sent them out. Someone who must have been very wise wrote down the things He said so that we can read about them today, many years after they were said.

The Báb told the Letters of the Living that they were the bearers of the Name of God in that Day. They were the ones who would tell everyone about the new Teacher God had sent. He told them that they must do only what they knew God wished them to do, because then people would know they were speaking the Truth and would listen to them.

That is a good thing for us to remember today—not to talk too much about what we are going to do. We can let our hands help other people and our feet run errands for them. Then everyone will see that we love God and are trying to be like Him. We will not even need to talk about it.

The Báb also told the Letters of the Living that God is very strong and that He would help them with all the difficult things they had to do. All they needed to do was to trust Him and know that He would help them.

This is the way He said it: "Arise in His name, put your trust wholly in Him, and be assured of ultimate victory."

No wonder they felt so strong and so joyful when they went away, even though they must have been sad at leaving Him. They scattered all over the land. Each one went first to his own home to give everyone there the Message.

Many people did not wish to listen. They thought the Letters of the Living were mistaken. Some of the Letters of the Living were put in prison, and some were beaten or stoned or punished in other cruel ways. They suffered a great deal.

But they remembered that the Báb had told them not to be afraid. Nothing could harm them until they had done their work. So they went right on teaching about the Promised One and about how much better the world was going to be because of Him.

Other people were glad to listen to the Letters of the Living. Here is the story of a man who listened to all they had to say.

One day at the house of a friend, this man heard Mullá Ḥusayn tell about the Promised One. When the talk was finished, the man eagerly asked Mullá Ḥusayn to tell him the name of the new Teacher.

"To inquire about that name and to divulge it are alike forbidden," Mullá Ḥusayn answered.

The man asked if it would be possible instead to try to discover the identity of the Promised One through prayer.

"The door of His grace," Mullá Ḥusayn replied, "is never closed before the face of him who seeks to find Him."

So the man asked his friend if he might go into another room at once so he could be alone and pray. He did not even want to wait until he went to his own home.

The man prostrated himself and began to pray. While he was praying, he remembered the face of a Young Man Whom he had seen praying at the shrine in Karbilá. Now, as he prayed, he saw this face again. In his vision the Young Man seemed to smile at him, and he

went forward to throw himself at the Young Man's feet. He was bending toward the ground when the vision disappeared. But the man felt sure that in his prayer he had seen the Promised One.

When the man ran out and told the others of his vision, Mullá Ḥusayn told him that he had, indeed, found the Báb.

"Declare not your vision to anyone," Mullá Ḥusayn said. "The time for it has not yet arrived."

Then Mullá Ḥusayn promised to meet the man later in Shíráz, if possible, where they would go together to see the Promised One.

The Message to Bahá'u'lláh

While the other Letters of the Living were teaching in their own homes, Mullá Ḥusayn went to the great city named Ṭihrán. Each day he would leave his room early in the morning and tell whomever would listen about the Promised One. Then he would return after sunset.

The Báb had told him something very important about Ṭihrán. These were His words: "A secret lies hidden in that city. When made manifest, it shall turn the earth into paradise." How often Mullá Ḥusayn must have thought and wondered about this.

Indeed he must have guessed part of the Secret. For he believed that in Ṭihrán he would find the other Promised One, Who was to come after the Báb and shed His Light upon the whole world. We learned in an earlier story that God was sending two divine Teachers instead of one. Knowing this, Mullá Ḥusayn must always have been watching for that other One.

Sometimes things happen in a very wonderful way in this world if we love God and try to do what He wants us to do. This is how Mullá Ḥusayn found out the secret about Ṭihrán.

One night at about twelve o'clock a man knocked at Mullá Ḥusayn's door. Mullá Ḥusayn was not expecting anyone, but he invited the man in and talked to him about the Báb. Mullá Ḥusayn asked the man what his name was and where he lived.

The visitor said he was from Núr, in the province of Mázindarán.

Mullá Ḥusayn knew that this was the home of Mírzá Buzurg, who had been well known for his character, his charm, and his many accomplishments. He wondered, now that Mírzá Buzurg had passed away, if there was anyone else in the family who was capable of the same accomplishments.

"Tell me," Mullá Ḥusayn said, "is there today among the family of the late Mírzá Buzurg . . . anyone who has proved himself capable of maintaining the high traditions of that illustrious house?"

"Yea," replied the man, "among his sons now living, one has distinguished Himself by the very traits which characterized His father."

Mullá Ḥusayn learned that this Son of Mírzá Buzurg was very wise and kind and generous and that He spent His time feeding the hungry, caring for the poor and those who were in trouble. Mullá Ḥusayn became very excited. He asked many questions about this distinguished Son. The more details he learned, the more excited he became. The visitor could not understand why.

"I presume you often meet Him?" Mullá Ḥusayn asked eagerly.

"I frequently visit His home," the man answered.

Mullá Ḥusayn asked him to deliver a scroll, or letter, to the Young Man at dawn and to bring back the answer if he should receive one.

Perhaps you have guessed that this Young Man of Núr was the other Promised One, the second divine Teacher Whom God was to send. He was Bahá'u'lláh. The messenger did not know Who He was, but just the sound of His voice as Bahá'u'lláh read the letter aloud made him happy. Then Bahá'u'lláh gave him a message and a gift of sugar and tea to carry back to Mullá Ḥusayn. Today this may seem a strange gift. But the people in Persia did not have much tea and sugar at that time, so they were always grateful to receive them.

When Mullá Ḥusayn received the message and the gift from Bahá'u'lláh, he was so excited and happy that he could hardly speak. He jumped up, took the gift from the man, and kissed it. He threw his arms about the messenger and said, "My dearly beloved friend! I pray that even as you have rejoiced my heart, God may grant you eternal felicity and fill your heart with imperishable gladness."

Still the man could not understand what had made Mullá Ḥusayn feel this way. Who was the Man to Whom he had taken the letter? He wondered. A few days later, just before Mullá Ḥusayn left Ṭihrán to go to another city, he called the messenger to him.

"Breathe not to anyone what you have heard and witnessed," Mullá Ḥusayn said. "Let this be a secret hidden within your breast." He explained that if he should tell others about the Young Man, people who were jealous would try to harm Him. Rather, it would be better to pray that God would take care of Him so that He might help the poor and all who were in trouble.

That is the way Mullá Ḥusayn found Bahá'u'lláh, the other Promised One. He knew, however, that he must not tell anyone about Bahá'u'lláh until the right time came. First they needed to hear that the Báb had come and that a new and beautiful Day had dawned.

Later, when the right time did come, the Báb told them about Bahá'u'lláh.

The Dream of Bahá'u'lláh's Father

One night, while Bahá'u'lláh was a little boy, His father had a strange dream about Him. In this dream Mírzá Buzurg saw his Son swimming in a great ocean. His body shone so brightly that even the water around Him was lighted up, and rays of light streamed from His head in all directions.

His hair was long and black, and, as He swam, it floated out on the water all around Him. As His father watched, a great number of fishes came, and each fish took in its mouth the end of one of the hairs of the

Boy's head. After that, wherever He swam, the fishes came, too. But they did not harm Him, and they did not prevent Him from swimming wherever He wished to go.

This dream was so very real to Bahá'u'lláh's father that he called a wise man to find out what it meant. The wise man told him that the ocean around his Son was the world. The many, many fishes that surrounded Him were the turmoil He would stir up among the people of the world. They would gather all around Him, but they would never be able to harm Him or keep Him from carrying out His work for God.

Bahá'u'lláh's father was very rich and lived in a great mansion with beautiful furniture and decorations. He was very kind and generous. He gave a great deal of money to help the poor people around him. Naturally he had many friends, and he was always happiest when he was doing something for someone else.

This went on for twenty years. Then trouble came. First a flood came down from the mountains near the village where he lived. The water swept along and carried away everything in its path. It carried away half of the mansion and all of its beautiful furniture and decorations.

Bahá'u'lláh's father was not as rich now, but still he went on helping those who needed him in every way he could. Then some of those whom he thought were his friends did all they could to take away the position he held. Still he remained calm and happy. He would not quarrel with them.

When Bahá'u'lláh grew up, He started to carry God's Message to the people. He did not tell them that He was a divine Teacher. It was not time. He told them about the Báb and the Message He brought. He went first to His old home. Here the people flocked to hear Him, and it seemed as if they could not hear enough of Him. Just listening to Bahá'u'lláh's voice made them love Him.

Some of those who had been leaders in the neighborhood asked Him to tell them about the great city where He had been. They wanted to hear about the Sháh of the country. But Bahá'u'lláh did not care for these things. He wanted to talk about God. He wished to tell them about the Báb and the New Day. He would go a long distance at any time to tell someone His Message.

Here is something very wonderful. People said that even the stones and the trees around Bahá'u'lláh were different because He was there. Everything seemed to grow better and seemed to proclaim the Beauty of God. Later, one of the names Bahá'u'lláh was known by was the Blessed Beauty.

So this is the way Bahá'u'lláh started to carry God's Message to the people. But still He did not tell them He was the second divine Teacher of Whom they had read in the Qur'án.

About this time the Báb was thinking of going on a long journey to the city of Mecca in Arabia. There was one reason why He did not wish to go. It was because the people of Persia needed so much to hear His Message. But one day He received a message from Mullá Ḥusayn saying that Bahá'u'lláh was teaching. This made Him very happy, for He knew that now He could go on His journey, and there would still be someone to tell about the Promised One and the New Day.

The Storm

In the days when the Báb and Bahá'u'lláh lived, boats did not have engines. They had to depend upon the wind to push their sails, and they could not travel very fast.

One day the Báb decided to go to the city of Mecca, which is where Muḥammad lived long ago. Every year many, many people who loved Muḥammad and who studied His Holy Book, the Qur'án, went to Mecca to pray. The Báb knew that He would meet many people there and to them He could give God's new Message. So He started out on a journey to Mecca with Quddús—one of the Letters of the Living—and His servant.

To get to this city they had to take a boat. Because there were only small boats, it took two long months to reach Mecca. Then, too, the weather was not good. A terrible storm came up. The big waves must have looked like mountains to the people in the small ship. It tossed them about so much that almost all of them became seasick.

But the Báb and Quddús did not seem uncomfortable at all. The rest of the travelers were afraid of the storm, but these two knew that God would take care of them. They feared nothing.

Every day Quddús would write down on paper the beautiful prayers and sayings that the Báb would dictate to him. Even when the storm was at its worst and the other travelers feared that the boat would sink and they would be drowned, the Báb and Quddús went right on with their work as if nothing were happening.

Then they had trouble in another way. The journey took so long that they found themselves at last without enough water to drink. The water in the ocean is not good to drink because it is salty. If you were to drink it, you would become all the more thirsty. The Báb wrote to someone that for days they had to satisfy their thirst with the juice of lemons instead of water.

Those who were on that little boat must have suffered a great deal. But something good came out of it. When the Báb saw their suffering, He prayed to God that ocean travel might be made easier. He prayed that there might not be so much danger.

God answered the Báb's prayer. In a very few years people learned how to make larger and better boats that storms could not harm as easily. They learned to use engines instead of sails so that the boats could go faster. And just think: Now it takes only a few days to make the same journey that took the Báb two months.

Today we know that it was the prayers of the Báb that made these changes, but at that time the people did not know this. They did not stop to think that it was God Who sent them all these good things.

In spite of their hard journey the Báb and Quddús at last safely reached the town on the seashore nearest to where they were going. From there they had to travel on camels across a hot, sandy desert before they reached Mecca, the holy city where Muḥammad had lived.

The sun can be very hot in the desert. There is no shade at all, and the sand grows so hot it is hard to travel across it. For this reason desert travelers always started very early in the morning, before the sun was up.

One morning the Báb stopped at a well and got off His camel for His morning prayer. He always remembered to pray because He knew that by praying He could stay close to God and know what He wished Him to do.

While the Báb was praying, a man who lived in the desert and wandered from place to place suddenly appeared near the travelers. Seeing them praying, he crept up softly, snatched the Báb's saddlebag, which was lying on the ground near Him, and ran away with it.

While the Báb and Quddús had been on the boat, Quddús had written down on paper many prayers and sayings of the Báb. These prayers were very precious, of

course, for they spoke of the Promised One and the New Day. They brought a great blessing to all who read them.

All of these papers were in the saddlebag that the desert man stole. The servant wanted to run after the thief, but the Báb motioned for him to come back.

It may seem very strange to us that the Báb allowed the man to carry away the papers that were so precious. But this is the reason the Báb gave: The man who ran away with the papers would carry them to different places in the desert where he went. In this way, many people would be able to read them and learn about the coming of the Promised One. And probably these people would not learn of it in any other way because they never went to the big cities far away.

"Grieve not, therefore, at his action," the Báb told His servant, "for this was decreed by God, the Ordainer, the Almighty."

The Story of Mullá Ṣádiq

After staying in Mecca for a time, the Báb and Quddús returned to their homes. On the way back the Báb told Quddús that when they reached their own country they would have to separate so they could teach in different places. They could not always be together.

The Báb warned Quddús that people would be very cruel to him. They would not listen to what he had to say, and finally they would kill him. The Báb promised, however, that a great joy would come to Quddús because he would die for God's Cause. He also promised that before Quddús died he would receive a great blessing. He would meet the second divine Teacher Whom God was sending.

We can imagine how happy that promise must have made Quddús. He did not fear anything the people might do to him. The Letters of the Living and others who loved the Báb were very brave because they knew this great secret about the Báb and the Teacher Who was to come.

Everything happened just as the Báb had said. While many people did not believe the Message and were very cruel, one of those who did believe Quddús was Mullá Ṣádiq, a teacher of the Qur'án. Wherever he went Mullá Ṣádiq told of the new Teacher, or Prophet, Whom God had sent. Eventually those who did not

wish to hear decided that he must be stopped. They arrested him and ordered that he be scourged, or whipped, a thousand strokes.

Mullá Ṣádiq was an old man, and no one thought he would be able to stand the lashing. But those who were watching had a great surprise. For what do you think? All of the time while he was being whipped and blood was running from his wounds, Mullá Ṣádiq was calm and smiling and seemed not even to be feeling it. The people could not understand.

It was true that Mullá Ṣádiq was not feeling the lashes. He told a friend afterward that the first seven strokes were very painful. But after that he actually wondered if the strokes were being applied to his own body, because he did not feel them. He even put his hand over his mouth to keep from laughing aloud, so happy was he.

"I can now realize," he said, "how the almighty Deliverer is able, in the twinkling of an eye, to turn pain into ease, and sorrow into gladness."

God is still able to take away our pain and make us happy if we turn to Him and trust Him as Mullá Ṣádiq did. And Mullá Ṣádiq was not the only one who was so happy to be serving the Báb that he did not mind it when people were cruel to him. Indeed, everyone who saw those who shared the Báb's Message marveled at how they could feel no fear at the terrible things that were done to them.

We know the secret, however. They were sure God was taking care of them at every moment and that nothing could happen that He did not wish for them. They were very happy because they loved the Báb so dearly, for it always makes us happy to love people.

The Báb Is Taken Prisoner

After Mullá Ṣádiq had been treated so cruelly, he and Quddús had to leave the city. The governor would not let them stay longer for he feared that the people would begin to believe their Message and turn against him. But Mullá Ṣádiq and Quddús did not mind going, because then they could give their Message in a new place.

After they had left the city, the governor decided he must make the Báb a prisoner to keep Him from talking to the people. He sent out a company of soldiers on horseback to find the Báb and bring Him back in chains. As they rode along in a very lonely place, they saw a Young Man wearing a green sash. He was on horseback, and His servant walked behind Him.

When the soldiers rode up, the Young Man saluted them and asked where they were going. The leader of the soldiers thought it best not to tell this stranger why they were there, so he replied that they were doing an errand for the governor.

At these words the Young Man smiled and said, "The governor has sent you to arrest Me. Here am I; do with Me as you please. By coming out to meet you, I have curtailed the length of your march, and have made it easier for you to find Me."

The leader was astonished at this answer. He could not understand why the Báb had come to meet them instead of running away when He saw them. The

leader did not want to take Him prisoner, so he pretended not to hear the Báb and started to leave.

But the Báb came up to him and declared that He had never said anything that was not the truth. He had no wish except to help other people. "I know that you are seeking Me," He said. "I prefer to deliver Myself into your hands, rather than subject you and your companions to unnecessary annoyance for My sake."

The leader was so overcome by these words that he got down from his horse and kissed the Báb's stirrup. He begged the Báb to escape from that place and not to let the governor take Him prisoner. He told the Báb that He could trust all the men not to tell where He had gone.

But the Báb refused to run away. He assured the leader that God would reward him for his kindness but that He could not run away. He told him that God would protect Him and that no one could harm Him until His work was done. And when it was done, He would be very happy to die for God, Whom He loved.

"Here am I," the Báb said. "Deliver Me into the hands of your master. Be not afraid, for no one will blame you."

So they went on together to the city, but the soldiers would not chain the Báb. All the way He rode ahead of the company of soldiers, as free as they were.

When they reached the city, the governor asked the Báb many questions and spoke to Him in such a way that it made the others who heard him very angry. The governor did not wish to do anything, however, that would make the people turn against him, so at last he let the Báb go. But before he freed Him, he made the Báb's uncle, who lived in the city, pay a great deal of money. He also made him sign a paper promising that, if the governor wanted the Báb again, this uncle would bring Him.

The Báb's mother and His wife, Khadíjih-Bagum, were with the uncle. Imagine how glad they all were to be together again. For a time the Báb lived with them very quietly, seeing no one except His closest friends.

The White Bird

This is the story of how a beautiful white bird helped someone to find the Báb. The name of the man who found Him was 'Abdu'l-Karím.

For many years, 'Abdu'l-Karím had wanted very much to know more about God and the great Teachers Whom He sent to the earth. He knew that to do this he must spend many years studying and praying.

All day he would study and talk over with his friends the things he had learned. Sometimes he studied far into the night. At the end of two years, those who were teachers of the Qur'án told him that he, too, was ready to teach. Of course, 'Abdu'l-Karím was very happy to hear this, and his father wished to give a feast for him. But 'Abdu'l-Karím asked him to wait for a few days.

Now this is the reason 'Abdu'l-Karím asked his father to wait: He did not feel that he was wise enough, or close enough to God, to teach

others about the Qur'án, even though he had studied it for two years. He knew that a teacher of the Qur'án should not make mistakes.

So he went to his room, and all night he prayed, asking God to tell him what to do. While he prayed he had a vision. He seemed to see a man talking to a great number of people. Their faces shone as if they were very happy. The man was telling them about a verse from the Qur'án. 'Abdu'l-Karím started toward the man in the dream, but just then he disappeared from sight.

The next day, 'Abdu'l-Karím was describing his vision to a wise man whom he knew. The wise man knew immediately that the noble person in 'Abdu'l-Karím's vision was Siyyid Káẓim, who was in Karbilá, for everyone who heard him loved him. This news made 'Abdu'l-Karím very happy. That same day he went to Karbilá, and there he saw Siyyid Káẓim. He was indeed the man 'Abdu'l-Karím had seen in his dream, and he was speaking about this same verse from the Qur'án. He was telling those who were listening about the Promised One.

"The Promised One," Siyyid Káẓim said, "lives in the midst of this people. The appointed time for His appearance is fast approaching. Prepare the way for Him, and purify yourselves so that you may recognize His beauty." He told them they should not rest for one moment until they found Him.

‘Abdu’l-Karím stayed in Karbilá for a time and then went home. Every day he was very busy, but at night he prayed and thought about the Promised One, asking God to help him find Him.

One night ‘Abdu’l-Karím had another vision. He saw before him a bird, white as snow, hovering above his head. It lighted on a tree beside him and in a very sweet voice said, “Are you seeking the Manifestation, O ‘Abdu’l-Karím? Lo, the year ’60.”

Then it flew away and left him very happy.

Every day ‘Abdu’l-Karím thought of his vision of the white bird and its strange message. A few years later, when he heard of the Báb, he hurried to Shíráz to see Him.

When ‘Abdu’l-Karím attained the presence of the Báb, he heard the Báb speak in a voice that sounded exactly like that of the white bird, saying the very same words the bird had said. Then ‘Abdu’l-Karím knew that he had found the Promised One, and he knelt at the Báb’s feet, too happy to speak. And, as the white bird had said, that was the year sixty.

The Plague

This is the story of how, one night, God saved the life of the Báb when the wicked governor had sent someone to take Him prisoner and planned to put Him to death.

This governor did not like the Báb because so many people flocked to hear Him and listen to His Message. The governor had Him watched wherever He went. Finally one night the governor called the chief constable of the city to him and said to go at once to the house in which the Báb was staying. Keeping out of sight, the constable was to climb the wall, reach the roof of the house and, from there, suddenly enter and arrest the Báb and all who were with Him. He was also to carry away any books or papers he found there.

The governor swore on that very night that he would have the Báb and His companions executed.

The chief constable did just as the governor had ordered. He arrested the Báb and His friends and started back to the home of the governor. But on the way a very strange thing happened.

When they reached the marketplace, they found people running this way and that, as if they were trying to get away from something. Everyone seemed too frightened to stop and talk. Then they saw a long train of coffins being hurried through the street, each followed by men and women shrieking and wailing.

The chief constable stopped one of these people to ask what had happened. He was told that on that very night a plague had broken out. Already over a hundred people had died. A plague is a very terrible sickness. It is so contagious that everyone near a person who has it may also be taken ill, and many of them die from it.

Greatly frightened, the chief constable ran to the home of the governor. But the doorkeeper told him that the governor had gone away, taking his family out of the city. One of his servants had died of the plague, and some members of his own family were ill.

The constable wondered what to do. He decided to take the Báb to his own home and keep Him prisoner there until the governor came back. On reaching his home, however, he heard the sound of crying and found that his son was sick and dying. In his despair the man threw himself at the feet of the Báb and begged Him to save the life of his son.

"Punish him not for the guilt which his father has committed," he begged. He told the Báb that he was very sorry for what he had done and would never again carry out the wicked wishes of the governor, even if he could find no other work and died of hunger.

The Báb was just about to wash His face and hands, as He always did before He prayed. He told the man to take some of the water to his son and ask him to drink it. This, He said, would save the boy's life.

The constable did as the Báb had said, and at once the son became well. Later the father sent a letter to the governor. He told him what had happened and begged him to let the Báb go before everyone in the city died of the plague.

The governor was frightened, and he wrote back that the Báb was to be freed at once. He could go wherever He pleased.

As for the wicked governor, he was dismissed from office by the Sháh and died poor and without friends. You see, the Báb's work was not yet finished, and not even a great man such as the governor could harm Him.

On the Road to Ṭihrán

By this time many, many people had heard the Báb's Message and followed Him in great crowds to hear Him speak. Everyone who was with Him loved Him dearly and would do all they could for Him. They did not feel this way about other leaders in the city. Most of these leaders were very proud and very cruel to those who did not think just as they did. These men grew jealous of the Báb, and they determined to get rid of Him.

Manúchihr Khán was the governor of the part of the country where the Báb was then teaching. He was friendly to the Báb and believed His Message. So when he heard of the wicked plan against the Báb, Manúchihr Khán made up his mind to save Him. He would pretend to send the Báb to the Sháh in Ṭihrán, and so get Him out of the city.

One day, about sunset, the Báb, with five hundred of the governor's own bodyguards, left the gate of the city and started toward Ṭihrán. They did not go to Ṭihrán, however. The governor had given orders that, every few miles, part of the guard should return to the city. At last only three were left with the Báb.

These three were the guards whom the governor trusted most. By a road on which they would meet few travelers, they brought the Báb back to the city, which they entered at dawn. They took Him to the governor's own house. Here He lived quietly for a while. Only a few close friends knew where He was.

Not long after this, Manúchihr Khán died. His nephew, who was not a friend of the Báb, became the new governor. The moment the nephew discovered that the Báb was still in the city, he wrote to the Sháh, who ordered that the Báb be sent to him at once.

The journey was made on horseback and took many days. Muḥammad Big was commander of the soldiers who were sent with the Báb. He and the other guards soon learned to love their Prisoner so much that, if the Báb had wished to escape, they would have let Him go gladly. But the Báb would not allow them to get into trouble because of Him. No one could be kinder than He was.

The Báb loved to be in the country. He was very happy when, one evening, they camped on a beautiful hill with orchards and meadows all about. A tent was pitched for Him so that He might be comfortable. While here, the Báb received from Bahá'u'lláh a letter and gifts that made Him so happy that everyone wondered, as they looked at His radiant face. Bahá'u'lláh, you remember, was the second divine Teacher Whom God was to send. But He had not, as yet, revealed Himself to the people.

One night while they were camped on the hill, it was suddenly discovered that the Báb's tent was empty. No one knew where He was. At first some of the guards were frightened, thinking that He had run away.

But Muḥammad Big spoke quietly to them: "He, no doubt, must have retired, in the silence of this moonlit night, to a place where He can seek undisturbed communion with God. He will unquestionably return to His tent. He will never desert us."

Sure enough, a few minutes later they saw Him coming alone from the direction of Ṭihrán.

"Did you believe Me to have escaped?" He asked.

The Báb looked so radiant and happy that Muḥammad Big threw himself at His feet. "Far be it from me to entertain such thoughts," he cried.

For two weeks they stayed in that lovely spot. Then a message came from the Sháh. The message said that the Sháh was leaving Ṭihrán and could not see the Báb at that time. The Báb was to be taken to the castle of Máh-Kú, where He was to stay until the Sháh again sent for Him.

The Báb knew that His enemies had asked the Sháh to do this. They believed that if the Báb were to be taken to this lonely spot, His friends would not be able to reach Him. They hoped that people would forget what they had heard about the coming of a new Teacher.

They did not understand that God does "whatsoever He willeth." No one could stop His Message from reaching the people.

When the Báb said good-bye to the soldiers, Muḥammad Big, with tears in his eyes, begged His forgiveness because he had not done enough for Him. But the Báb told the soldier that He would always remember him for his kindness and that all who heard about him would bless him.

The other soldiers also kissed the Báb's feet and, with tears in their eyes, asked Him to bless them. He thanked each of them warmly for their kindness.

The Castle of Máh-Kú

In the last story we heard how the Sháh ordered that the Báb be shut up in the castle of Máh-Kú. The Sháh and others near him thought that doing this would make the people forget the Báb and His Message.

The castle of Máh-Kú was high up on a mountain in a very lonely part of the country. At the foot of the mountain was a small town. The people who lived there were rough and quarrelsome. There was only one road from the castle, and this road led through the town to a gate that was always closed and guarded.

'Alí Khán had charge of the castle. 'Alí Khán was a soldier who was very stern and unfriendly to the Báb and the two friends who were allowed to live with Him. No other friends were allowed, even in the town.

The Báb was so kind and gentle, however, that it was not long before these rough people began to love Him just as others did. Early in the morning many would come to the foot of the mountain where they could look up at His window. They hoped they might see Him for a moment. Then He would bless their work for the day.

But 'Alí Khán remained very unfriendly and would let none of the Báb's friends come to Him.

Then one day a strange thing happened, something that showed how very wonderful the Báb was.

The Báb and the two who were with Him in the castle heard a knock at the door. Opening it, they saw 'Alí Khán waiting to come in. But it was a very different 'Alí Khán. Before, he had been very proud and cruel looking. Now he seemed much gentler, and there was a look of surprise on his face. He even trembled as he stepped into the room in which the Báb sat. A moment later, to the great astonishment of the two friends, he threw himself at the Báb's feet. They could hardly believe their eyes.

"Deliver me from my perplexity," 'Alí Khán begged, looking at the Báb. Then he told of a strange thing that had happened to him, something he could not understand.

That morning at dawn, 'Alí Khán had been riding through the country outside the town. It was so early that no one was about, except one man who was standing beside the river, praying. 'Alí Khán went closer and, to his astonishment, saw that the man was the Báb. 'Alí Khán started toward Him to rebuke Him for leaving the castle, but the Báb was so deep in prayer that He did not hear him. Then 'Alí Khán decided that he would leave the Báb there for a time. He would hurry back to the castle and punish the guards for allowing the Báb to leave.

When 'Alí Khán reached the town he was very surprised to find the gate locked. Also, the door of the castle was closed and locked, just as he had left it. And when the door was opened, there was the Báb, seated before him. Imagine how astonished ‘Alí Khán must have been, for he had just left the Báb beside the river.

“I am utterly confounded,” he said to the Báb. “I know not whether my reason has deserted me.” ‘Alí Khán was afraid he was losing his mind.

“What you have witnessed is true and undeniable,” the Báb answered. He went on to explain that God wished to show ‘Alí Khán that the Báb’s Message was true. God wanted him to see how wonderful it was and to love this divine Teacher Whom He had sent.

From that day on ‘Alí Khán was so changed that the people of the town hardly knew him. Instead of being cruel and proud, he was kind and gentle. The gate of the castle was still closed at night, but during the day it was left open. Everyone who wished to see the Báb was allowed to enter. Every day ‘Alí Khán brought Him fresh fruit or something else that He might like to eat.

While the Báb was a prisoner in the castle, He wrote a very important holy book called the Persian Bayán. In it He laid down the laws of God that the people were to obey. And in it He told about the next divine Teacher Whom God was to send. He urged everyone to try to find Him.

When we read this true story about the Báb, it helps us understand how God brings good out of everything, even though it may not seem so at first. The Sháh thought that when he sent the Báb to Máh-Kú he was sending Him to a place where He would not be able to see or talk to anyone. But all the people who lived in the mountains around the castle heard the Báb's Message and became His friends. And He wrote a very great book that became the Law for His day.

Alí Khán's Dream

One day while the Báb was still being held prisoner in the castle of Máh-Kú, Mullá Ḥusayn came to visit. How very happy Mullá Ḥusayn must have been to know that he was going to see the Báb again. We know that the visit meant a great deal to him because he walked all the way, and it was a long, hard journey. His friends wished to give him many things to make the journey easier, but he would take none of them. This is the story of how he came to the castle of Máh-Kú.

The night before Mullá Ḥusayn arrived was the eve of the New Year. On that night 'Alí Khán, who had charge of the castle, had a dream. In his dream he heard that Muḥammad was to visit the Báb on New Year's Day. Feeling very excited, 'Alí Khán ran out to meet Him. 'Alí Khán walked toward the river, and as he reached the bridge he saw two men coming toward him, one walking before the other. He thought the first one was Muḥammad. Running forward, 'Alí Khán was about to throw himself at His feet when he awoke from the dream.

'Alí Khán felt happier than he had ever felt in his life. It seemed as if he were in heaven. So real did it all seem that he felt sure it was more than a dream.

'Alí Khán said his morning prayer and put his richest clothes on. Then he started out to the spot where, in his dream, he thought he had seen Muḥam-mad. He ordered his servants to saddle three of his best and swiftest horses and take them at once to the bridge.

It was very early in the morning. The sun had just come up when 'Alí Khán walked alone toward the river. And at the bridge, just as he had dreamed, he saw two men coming, walking one before the other.

'Alí Khán fell at the feet of the one whom he thought was Muḥammad and begged him and his companion to ride the horses the rest of the way.

"Nay," he said, "I have vowed to accomplish the whole of my journey on foot. I will walk to the summit of this mountain and will there visit your Prisoner."

The visitor was not Muḥammad, as 'Alí Khán had dreamed, but Mullá Ḥusayn. 'Alí Khán followed him until they reached the gate of the castle. There the Báb stood, waiting. At the sight of Him, Mullá Ḥusayn stopped and bowed low, but the Báb took him in His arms. Then, taking him by the hand, He led Mullá Ḥusayn into the castle, where they celebrated together the feast of Naw-Rúz, or the New Year.

Until that time none of the Báb's friends—except the two who lived with Him—had been allowed to spend the night in the castle. But that day 'Alí Khán went to the Báb and said, "If it be Your desire to retain Mullá Ḥusayn with You this night, I am ready to abide by Your wish, for I have no will of my own. However long You desire him to stay with You, I pledge myself to carry out Your command."

This shows how much 'Alí Khán had changed.

While Mullá Ḥusayn was in the castle, the Báb said to him, "A few days after your departure from this place, they will transfer Us to another mountain. Ere you arrive at your destination, the news of Our departure from Máh-Kú will have reached you."

It happened as the Báb had said. He was sent to another castle because 'Alí Khán had become so friendly to Him and because so many of His friends had found Him. At one of the places where Mullá Ḥusayn stopped, he heard about the change.

As for Mullá Ḥusayn, he walked all the way back to his home, just as he had walked to the castle of Máh-Kú.

Ṭáhirih

We have heard about a great many men who heard the Message of the Báb and set out to tell others about Him. Now we are going to hear about an extraordinary woman who also traveled about to give His Message. Her name was Ṭáhirih, and she was very beautiful, intelligent, and courageous. She wrote marvelous poems. Perhaps someday you will read some of them.

At that time the women of Persia did not go about freely among people as the men did. When it was necessary for them to go out on the street, they wore veils over their faces so they could not be seen. Ṭáhirih, too, wore such a veil for many years. After a while, however, she did not believe it was necessary for women to do this, and she was the first to go out of her home without one. Later you will hear about how she first appeared without it.

Ṭáhirih was one of the Letters of the Living, the first eighteen disciples, or followers, of the Báb. All were men except Ṭáhirih, and she did not even have to see the Báb to believe in Him! As soon as she heard the Message from someone else, she knew that it was true. She sent a letter to the Báb at once. In this letter she told Him how happy she was to receive the Message and that she knew it to be true. The Báb answered this letter and named her one of the Letters of the Living.

From this time on, Ṭáhirih spent her days telling everyone who would listen about the Báb. But it was not very long before the people who did not like the Báb began to try to harm Ṭáhirih. They wanted to stop her from telling others about Him. And at last she was made a prisoner in her father's home and allowed to see no one.

Ṭáhirih knew they wished to kill her, just as they had wished to kill others of the Báb's disciples. But she was not afraid of them because she knew that God would take care of her.

She told those who were keeping her prisoner that she would prove the Message she was giving was really from God. She told them that if her Message was true, God would free her in nine days from the house where she was locked up and guarded. Of course they did not believe this was possible, but we shall see what happened.

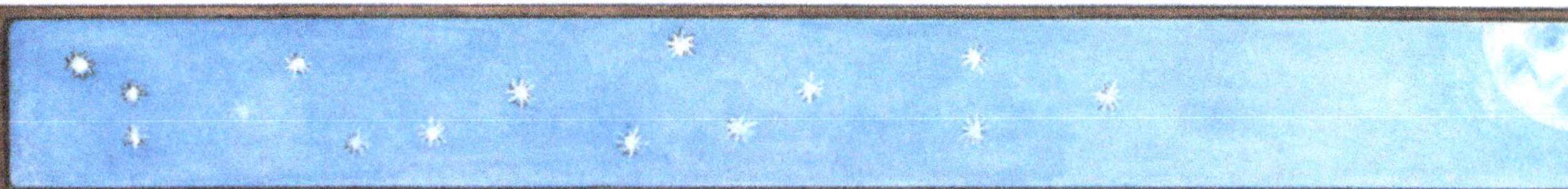

At this time Bahá'u'lláh decided Ṭáhirih should be allowed to go free. He was determined to show the people that the Message she was telling people about was truly truly from God. So Bahá'u'lláh sent for one of His friends and told him that he was to take Ṭáhirih to Bahá'u'lláh's own house in the city of Ṭihrán.

This is how it was done. The wife of the man who was to take Ṭáhirih to Ṭihrán disguised herself as a beggar so that no one would recognize her. Then she went to the house where Ṭáhirih was being kept prisoner and gave her a letter from Bahá'u'lláh. This letter told Ṭáhirih exactly what to do. The woman waited at the door of the house until Ṭáhirih joined her. Then they hurried back to her husband. Of course Ṭáhirih, too, was disguised so that no one would know her and stop her.

In those days there were high walls around the city so that enemies could not enter. The man had brought three horses and left them in a safe place outside the city wall. He and the two women were able to get to the horses without being seen. Then they followed a lonely road until they came to Ṭihrán at dawn. And so Ṭáhirih safely reached the house of Bahá'u'lláh.

In the meantime, when it was discovered that Ṭáhirih had escaped, everyone was filled with wonder. Even her friends could not imagine where she had gone or how she had gotten away. The whole night long they searched the houses all around, but they did not find her.

Then they remembered what she had told them—that if her message about the Báb was true, God would free her from prison within nine days. Now she was gone, and the nine days were not yet up. Many people believed the Message and became followers of the Báb because of what had happened.

All this time Ṭáhirih was very happy in the home of Bahá'u'lláh. He had not yet announced that He was the second divine Teacher Whom God was sending. But Ṭáhirih was so good and lived so close to God that she knew His secret. Imagine how happy it must have made her to live in His house.

The New Order

All this time the Báb and Bahá'u'lláh and Their followers had been obeying the laws that had been set down in the Qur'án. You see, when one of God's divine Teachers comes to us, He leaves directions, or laws, for us in a Holy Book. Muḥammad had left directions in the Qur'án.

After many years, however, some of the laws in these Holy Books must be changed because people have grown wiser and no longer need them. God sends a new Teacher to make new laws and leave new directions.

Now, in the days we have been hearing about, it was time for some of the laws to be changed. They were no longer needed. This story tells about the way one was changed.

Ṭáhirih had been living in the home of Bahá'u'lláh. After a time, however, He decided to send her to another city. This was not easy to do because the gates of the city were guarded. Women were not allowed to leave the city without a letter or permit.

However, the guards did not stop Ṭáhirih and those who were with her. They did not even ask where they were going. This shows what Bahá'u'lláh's wish was able to do.

A few days later Bahá'u'lláh, too, left the city and traveled in the same direction. And not long after, they were met by Quddús, who had come to welcome His Holiness, Bahá'u'lláh.

All the people of the neighborhood were very excited over the presence of Bahá'u'lláh and Quddús. Some were so glad that they were ready to do anything for them. Others were filled with hate and wished to harm them.

That is the way it always is at the coming of one of God's Teachers. People either love Them very, very dearly, or they fear Them and wish Them harm. You see, it depends upon what is in each person's heart. If hearts are kind and good, they love these Teachers. If they are wicked, they do not wish to hear Them.

It was now the beginning of summer. Bahá'u'lláh rented three gardens—one for Ṭáhirih, one for Quddús, and one for Himself. When the friends learned about this, many came to be near Them. Finally eighty-one people had gathered. All were guests of Bahá'u'lláh.

One day while the friends were sitting together, a messenger came from Ṭáhirih. The message said that she would like to have Quddús come to her. Because

Quddús did not wish to leave Bahá'u'lláh, he refused her invitation. Again the messenger came with the same message.

"She insists on your visit," he said. "If you persist in your refusal, she herself will come to you."

Quddús was about to say no again when, at that very moment, Ṭáhirih herself came in. And to everyone's great astonishment, she was not wearing a veil.

It is hard for us to imagine how shocked they were to see her, or how courageous she was to do this, for women of Persia at that time always wore veils when they were away from their own homes. Everyone was aghast. To look at a woman's shadow was considered improper. To gaze at her uncovered face was scandalous. The men were filled with fear, anger, and confusion. One man was so disturbed that he cut his own throat and ran away, shrieking.

But Ṭáhirih was so sure she was doing what was right that her face shone with joy. One story tells us that she cried, "I am the blast of the trumpet, I am the call of the bugle. . . . I would awaken sleeping souls." By this she meant that the time had come for the old laws about women to be changed.

As Ṭáhirih spoke to them, her words were so like those in the Qur'án that all were surprised and interested. It was then that Bahá'u'lláh gave her the name of Ṭáhirih, which means "the Pure One." From then on, the women of the East began to be more free in many ways. How grateful they must have been to this beautiful, courageous woman.

And from that day on, the lives and habits of the followers of the Báb were changed in many ways. They knew that the old order, or the old way of doing things, had gone; and the New Order, or the New Day, had come. When they went on to another city, Quddús and Ṭáhirih traveled together in the same howdah, or carriage.

Muḥammad-'Alí's Vision

Do you remember the story of how the Báb was made prisoner in the castle of Máh-Kú? After a time He was sent to another place and then to another. But His enemies could not keep people away from Him. They only came to love Him and follow Him more and more.

One young man named Muḥammad-'Alí heard the Báb's Message and wished to go to Him, even though the Báb was then in prison. Muḥammad-'Alí said he would be glad to die for Him.

His stepfather, however, would not allow Muḥammad-'Alí to leave the city. He locked the young man in the house and kept a strict watch over him, for he did not believe the Báb's Message, and he was afraid his son had lost his mind.

One day a surprising thing happened. Up to this time Muḥammad-'Alí had wept most of the time because he could not go to the Báb. Now, however, he had suddenly become very joyous. Instead of weeping he was smiling.

Would you like to know the reason for this change? This is it: For an entire day Muḥammad-'Alí had prayed to be allowed to see the face of the Báb. He prayed so hard that at last he seemed to become unconscious. Then he had a vision.

In this vision he heard the voice of the Báb calling him. The voice told him to rise, and when he did so he seemed to be looking into the smiling eyes of the Báb. Filled with joy and thankfulness, the young man rushed forward and fell at the Báb's feet.

"Rejoice," the Báb said, "the hour is approaching when, in this very city, I shall be suspended before the eyes of the multitude and shall fall a victim to the fire of the enemy. I shall choose no one except you to share with Me the cup of martyrdom. Rest assured that this promise which I give you shall be fulfilled."

Do you know what the Báb meant by these words? He meant this: After a while He, the Báb, would be put to death in that very city, with many people watching. At that time He would choose Muḥammad-'Alí to die with Him. That was His promise. You see, it would be a very great blessing and honor to die with the Báb, and all of His friends wished they could be the ones to do so. But only this young man, He said, was to be chosen.

It was this promise that made Muḥammad-'Alí so happy. From that day on, nothing could make him sad. He said he felt as if he were living in an ocean of joy. The Báb's voice kept ringing in his ears, and he seemed to see Him many times during the day and night. Muḥammad-'Alí's father could not understand the change in him, but at last he allowed him to go free.

From that day forward Muḥammad-'Alí lived quietly and happily with his family and his friends, and everyone loved him so much that when he died with the Báb, as he had been promised, all the people in the city wept for him.

The Trial of the Báb

By this time greater and greater crowds of people came to hear the Báb's Message. But the city leaders and their friends were almost always His enemies and wished Him harm.

Some of them felt very proud because they had studied more than other people, and so they could explain the Qur'án to them. Others were proud because they had a great deal of money or a high position in the government. These people were all afraid that if most of the people of Persia became followers of the Báb they themselves would not be so important. They might lose their money or their position. And so, everywhere the Báb went, they treated Him cruelly.

All who were with Him for a while, however, became His friends. Even the animals seemed to love Him, for if they had been fierce, they became gentle in His presence. Here is a story of what once happened.

The prince in whose home the Báb was staying wished to see if the Báb was brave. So he gave Him a very wild horse to ride. The groom who had charge of the horse went to the Báb secretly and asked Him not to ride this horse. He told Him that the horse had thrown everyone who had tried to ride it. The Báb thanked the groom but told him to leave Him in the hands of God. All would be well. When the Báb quietly walked up and began to pat the horse and put His foot in the stirrup, the animal stood still and let Him get on its back. The horse continued to be gentle until the Báb had returned from His ride.

So many people followed the Báb on His way to the city of Tabríz that His enemies, the religious leaders, would not let Him come into the city. They feared there would be trouble. They sent word to the Báb that He must camp outside the city. Then they held a meeting and sent for Him to come before them. They intended to question Him.

When the Báb arrived He found that every chair except one was taken. People pressed in on every side. As the Báb walked through the crowd and took the empty chair, suddenly the people seemed to feel His power. Everyone had been talking together noisily. Suddenly a deep and mysterious silence fell upon them. Not one person dared to breathe a single word.

At last the stillness was broken by one of the leaders. "Whom do you claim to be," he asked the Báb, "and what is the message which you have brought?"

"I am," the Báb replied three times, "I am, I am, the promised One! I am the One whose name you have for a thousand years invoked, at whose mention you have risen, whose advent you have longed to witness, and the hour of whose Revelation you have prayed God to hasten."

You see, they had been waiting for Him, and yet when He came they would not receive Him. They asked Him many questions, all of which He answered, but still they refused to believe that He was the Promised One. They treated Him shamefully and again sent Him to prison.

The news of this gathering traveled all over the land and made the Báb's friends want to do more and more for Him. Many who had not been His followers thought that the religious leaders had treated Him unfairly, and they, too, became His friends. Whatever they tried to do against Him did not succeed. It only made more people love Him.

Fort Ṭabarsí

Do you remember Mullá Ḥusayn? He was the first one to recognize that the Báb was the Promised One. And ever since that important night in Shíráz, Mullá Ḥusayn had been telling everyone about the Báb.

One day a messenger came to Mullá Ḥusayn, bringing him the Báb's turban and telling him to go and help Quddús. Quddús was the one who had accompanied the Báb on His journey to the city of Mecca.

As soon as Mullá Ḥusayn received the message, he mounted his horse and set forth with two hundred and two companions. Wherever they stopped, they gave people the Message of the New Day and selected some of those who believed it to go with them on their journey.

Once, when they had stopped to rest, Mullá Ḥusayn said to his companions, "Whoever is unprepared for the great trials that lie before us, let him now repair to his home and give up the journey." He repeated the warning several times, then said, "I, together with seventy-two of my companions, shall suffer death for the sake of the Well-Beloved. Whoso is unable to renounce the world, let him now, at this very moment, depart, for later on he will be unable to escape."

Mullá Ḥusayn meant that those who were afraid to die for God should leave before it was too late. Twenty of them left and returned to their homes. Then Mullá Ḥusayn told the rest to leave behind everything that they owned, except their horses and their swords, so that people would see they did not want the things of this world. They only wished to teach God's Message.

Many times members of this little band were forced to fight for their lives. But their leader would never let them be the first to fight. They fought only when they had to. Everyone was amazed at Mullá Ḥusayn's bravery, and a mysterious strength seemed to come to him whenever it was needed. His enemies trembled even at the sound of his name.

The night before they arrived at the shrine of Shaykh Ṭabarsí, the keeper of the shrine dreamed that Mullá Ḥusayn had come there with a great number of people. He dreamed that they stayed there, winning every battle against their enemies. And one night the Prophet of God joined them. The Prophets, you know, are the divine Teachers we have been hearing about. When Mullá Ḥusayn came the next morning, the caretaker knew that this was the person he had seen in his dream with all the people. The guardian of the shrine told Mullá Ḥusayn about his dream.

"All that you have witnessed," Mullá Ḥusayn told the keeper of the shrine, "will come to pass."

Mullá Ḥusayn decided to build a fort that enclosed the shrine and at once set his men to work. Many times they had to stop and fight the people of the neighboring towns who tried to harm them. But always they drove their enemies away. At last the fort was finished.

Just after it was finished, Mullá Ḥusayn received word that Bahá'u'lláh was coming to visit them. In the dream of the guardian of the shrine, the Prophet of God came to join them. This Prophet was Bahá'u'lláh.

Those who were with Mullá Ḥusayn did not know at that time Who Bahá'u'lláh was, and they did not understand why their leader was so happy that he even forgot they were present. When Bahá'u'lláh arrived, no one could sit down until Mullá Ḥusayn gave the word, and he forgot until Bahá'u'lláh Himself told them to be seated.

Bahá'u'lláh told them that He was satisfied with the fort and that only one thing was lacking to make it perfect: Quddús must be with them. Quddús was in prison, but Bahá'u'lláh told Mullá Ḥusayn to send six men for him and that he would be allowed to join them.

Before Bahá'u'lláh left them He said, "Whatever may befall, victory is yours, a victory which is complete and certain."

When Bahá'u'lláh had gone, Mullá Ḥusayn sent six men for Quddús. He then told the others that they must treat Quddús as they would treat the Báb Himself. "As to myself," he added, "you must consider me as his lowly servant."

Quddús arrived at the fort during the night. When a messenger came to say that he was near, Mullá Ḥusayn and one hundred men went to meet him. Each man carried two lighted candles so that the forest was illuminated about them. As Quddús rode among them back to the fort, they sang a song of praise to God.

Every day after that, no matter how fiercely the enemy attacked the fort, Quddús always kept his time to pray with his companions around him. Nothing could keep him from speaking in this way to God, Whom he loved and trusted.

The Siege

For many weeks Quddús, Mullá Ḥusayn, and their companions were kept inside the fort by those who wished to harm them. They could not go out for food, for everyone who did so was shot. At last, even water became scarce.

When someone spoke to Quddús about this, he said, "God willing, this very night a downpour of rain will overtake our opponents, followed by a heavy snowfall. . . ."

Sure enough, that very night a heavy rain fell and ruined the enemy's ammunition. Enough water was gathered within the fort to last the men for a long time. On the next night there came a fall of snow so heavy that no one in the neighborhood of the fort could remember one like it, even in the middle of winter. So you see, that which caused a great deal of trouble to the enemy was a blessing to those in the fort.

The little band inside the fort knew that the large army outside was getting ready to attack them. So Quddús decided to rush out at them suddenly and try to drive them back or scatter them. Two hours after sunrise he and two others mounted their horses and rode out of the fort. The rest followed on foot.

As soon as they were out, they all shouted as loudly as they could, "O Lord of the Age!" This was one of the names of the Báb.

The great roar of their shouts and the glitter of the sun on their weapons frightened the enemy. The soldiers ran in all directions, leaving behind all their possessions, and not one of the men from the fort lost his life.

Quddús would not let his men follow those who were running away. He did not wish to harm anyone if it was not necessary. He just wanted to show them the power of God so that the people would allow him and his followers to give the Message of the Báb.

This same thing happened again and again. The tiny army in the fort would suddenly rush out, shouting "O Lord of the Age!" And always they were able to drive back the large, trained army that had come against them. In one of these battles Quddús was struck by a bullet and wounded in the mouth and throat. But Mullá Ḥusayn, with a sword in each hand, and followed by the rest of his men, drove the enemy back. Then they returned to the fort with Quddús, who was soon well again.

At one time Bahá'u'lláh started to join them. But He and those with Him were captured by the enemy and held prisoners for a time. Bahá'u'lláh was treated very well, not at all like a prisoner. In this way He was prevented from joining those in the fort. And it is a good thing He was, or He might have perished with them. This is how God takes care of His Cause.

It was as a result of one of those battles that Mullá Ḥusayn lost his life. It happened in this way. During the fighting, Mullá Ḥusayn's horse became entangled in a tent rope, and before it could get away, a bullet struck Mullá Ḥusayn in the chest. He fell from his horse, staggered a few steps, and dropped to the ground. Two of his companions carried him back to the fort.

There in the fort a strange thing happened. Although Mullá Ḥusayn was unconscious when they carried him in, Quddús told the others to leave them alone. He said he wished to talk to Mullá Ḥusayn.

Through a crack in the door, one of the men saw what happened. As soon as the two were alone, Quddús called Mullá Ḥusayn, who rose and sat at his feet. The others could hear him answering questions and talking.

They talked together in this way for two hours. Then the door opened, and Quddús came out. "I have bade my last farewell to him," he said.

He explained that he had told Mullá Ḥusayn many things he had not been ready to hear before. When the others went in, Mullá Ḥusayn was dead. There was a smile on his face, and he looked as if he had just fallen asleep.

Mullá Ḥusayn was buried near the shrine of Shaykh Ṭabarsí. Later the bodies of the thirty others who had died in that battle were laid to rest in the same place. They had all given their lives for God's Cause, which was the most glorious thing they could possibly do.

The Death of Quddús

After Mullá Ḥusayn left them, very hard times came to the fort of Shaykh Ṭabarsí. The enemy would let no one in or out, so that they could get nothing to eat. But with Quddús there they were so happy that they forgot they were hungry. If they began to feel weak and ill, they had only to look at his joyous face and hear his voice to feel strong again and able to do anything.

One day a cannonball from the enemy fell inside the fort and rolled to where Quddús stood. He showed no fear whatever, but only pushed the ball aside with his foot. Then he told his companions that they need not be afraid of the enemy. Each one of them had an appointed time to die. Until that time, nothing could hurt them. But if they should let the sound of the guns make them afraid, they would deprive themselves of God's protection. If they were afraid, they could not be protected. They had to know that God would care for them.

Not long after this the enemy decided that they would never be able to capture the fort and those brave souls in it. Then they decided to do a terrible thing. They decided to promise those in the fort that they might return safely to their homes. Then, when they had left the shelter of the fort, they could do as they pleased with them.

The captain of the enemy forces sent a copy of the Qur'án to those in the fort and promised they would be protected if they would come out. Quddús felt the captain was not telling the truth, but, because he had pledged by the Qur'án, they must trust him.

So they all marched out. Quddús wore the green turban that the Báb had sent to him and rode a horse sent by the prince who was at the head of the enemy's army.

But everything happened just as Quddús had feared. The enemies had made a promise without any intention of keeping it. The fort was completely destroyed. All of the companions of Quddús were either put to death or sold as slaves.

As for Quddús, the prince for a time protected him. Later, however, the religious leaders, who had always been his enemies, ordered him to come before them and answer their questions.

The prince knew that they meant to put Quddús to death, so at last he said, "I wash my hands of all responsibility for any harm that may befall this man. You are free to do what you like with him. You will yourselves be answerable to God on the Day of Judgment."

The prince then called for his horse and rode away, leaving Quddús in the hands of his enemies. It was a cowardly thing to do.

They put Quddús to death in such a cruel way that, when the Báb heard about it and about what had happened at the fort, tears rained from His eyes. For nine days the Báb would see none of His friends, and He was unable to write for six long months.

But Quddús was not angry with those who put him to death. In his suffering he was heard to say, "Forgive, O my God, the trespasses of this people. Deal with them in Thy mercy, for they know not what we already have discovered and cherish. . . . Show them, O God, the way of Truth, and turn their ignorance into faith."

You see, Quddús felt sorry for them because they did not know about the Báb and Bahá'u'lláh as he did.

And so Quddús died, as Mullá Ḥusayn had, and as the Báb knew that later He would die, for God's Caùse. But all the time more and more people believed the Báb's Message, and that was all that they cared for or thought about.

The Story of Vaḥíd

Vaḥíd was another brave leader who believed the Báb's Message and told the people about it. Because of his faith the governor sent a regiment of soldiers to fight him and scatter his friends. When Vaḥíd heard them coming, he told one of his followers to take six men and go out to meet them. That may sound like very few men to meet the trained soldiers, but what happened next was truly amazing.

Vaḥíd told his men to shout seven times the words "Alláh-u-Akbar." This means "God is Most Great." At the seventh time, they were to rush forth and scatter the enemy. The seven men had such strong faith that they seemed suddenly to become much more powerful. They had no trouble in scattering the regiment of soldiers.

That night, Vaḥíd told those who were with him to go quietly away. His wife and children were sent to the home of her father so that they might be safe. Then, in the middle of the night, Vaḥíd left the city without anyone seeing him. His two oldest sons and two other companions went with him.

During the day, they hid in the mountains, and Vaḥíd's brother, who lived in that neighborhood, sent them food. That same day a company of the governor's soldiers, who were hunting for Vaḥíd, searched his brother's house, but of course they did not find him.

Vaḥíd and his companions traveled on, stopping at every village to give their message of the new Teachers and the New Day that had dawned.

At last they reached a place called Nayríz. Here Vaḥíd gave his message again, and more and more people came to hear it. There were so many people that Vaḥíd feared the governor would again send the soldiers against them. So he told those who had come with him to go into an old fort not far away and make it as strong as possible. Later he, too, came to live in the fort.

Sure enough, the governor would not let Vaḥíd and his companions live in peace. Again and again the governor's army attacked the fort, where there were only seventy-two men. Many of these seventy-two were either old men or young boys. And yet every time they rushed forth with their cry of "Alláh-u-Akbar" they frightened the enemy and scattered them. The same thing had happened in the siege of S͟haykh Ṭabarsí.

Like the leader of the enemy at Ṭabarsí, the governor at last decided that he would not be able to win in a fair battle against the little handful of men and boys in the fort. He felt that the only way he could win was to trick them. So he sent a message to Vaḥíd, telling him that he and his friends had not understood what Vaḥíd wanted. They thought he wanted to be a great leader in the city.

Now, they said, they knew that he only wanted to deliver the Message of the Báb. If he would come to them, they would make peace, and he and his followers could go free. If he would not do this, they would all be killed.

Like Quddús at Ṭabarsí, Vaḥíd knew they did not mean this, but he felt that he should take the chance to give the Báb's Message again. He and the few he took with him to the meeting were treated well. Their enemies dared do nothing while Vaḥíd's friends were still in the fort. So they made Vaḥíd send a letter to the fort, telling them to come to him at the headquarters of the army.

Knowing that the governor was planning to kill them when they came out, Vaḥíd secretly wrote a second letter telling them to stay where they were. The messenger was to destroy the first letter and take the second to the fort.

But this messenger was not true to Vaḥíd. He destroyed the second letter and took the first to the fort. And when those in the fort came out, they were scattered and most of them were killed.

After that the governor and his friends were no longer afraid, and they put to death Vaḥíd and those who had come with him. That is the way another brave man died for God's Cause. But he had made many, many friends who would carry on his work.

The Martyrdom of the Báb

Do you know what the word "martyrdom" means? It means to die for God's Cause. Those who are put to death because they are trying to teach others about God and what He wishes are called martyrs. All of the people we have been hearing about were martyrs. They died trying to tell people that a new divine Teacher, the Báb, had come.

Perhaps you might think that after so many of the Báb's followers had been killed, people would be afraid to listen and say that they believed. That was not the case with most of them, however. When they saw that so many people were glad to die for this Cause, they knew it must be true. Always more and more became followers of the Báb. No one had been able to harm Him. Wherever He went, most of the people loved Him and were ready to die for Him. Some even kissed the dust where He had walked.

Now the Grand Vazír hated the Báb. The Grand Vazír was the man who was nearest to the Sháh and who helped him decide what to do. This was a very important position. Unfortunately the Grand Vazír did not understand the Báb's Message. And he did not want the Báb to talk with the Sháh for fear that he, too, would come to believe the new Message. The Grand Vazír feared that, if this happened, he might lose his position.

So he decided that in some way the Báb must be put to death. He thought that the Báb's followers would be afraid to continue without Him and that the Cause would then die out. He sent a soldier to the Báb's prison. This soldier was to bring the Báb to Tabríz.

The Báb knew what was happening, though He was a prisoner far away. Forty days before the message came, He collected all of His writings. With them He put His pen-case, His seals and agate rings, and sent them by one of the Letters of the Living to Aḥmad, His amanuensis, or secretary. The Báb urged the messenger to take the greatest care of these things and to tell no one about them except Aḥmad.

When the things were given to Aḥmad, he found among them a letter from the Báb. In this letter the Báb said that these precious things were to be taken to Bahá'u'lláh. Aḥmad at once set out for the city of Ṭihrán. There he gave the things to Bahá'u'lláh.

Three days after the Báb was taken to Tabríz an order came from the Grand Vazír saying that the Báb was to be put to death on that very day in the courtyard of the barracks, the place where the soldiers stayed. And anyone who admitted to being a follower of the Báb was also to be put to death.

The man in whose house the Báb was staying refused to have anything to do with this despicable order. So another order came that the Báb and His amanuensis were to be taken to one of the rooms in the barracks. Ten men were to guard the door of His room.

There was great turmoil in the streets as the Báb and Ḥusayn, His amanuensis, were led through them. When they came near the barracks, a young man suddenly forced his way through the crowd and flung himself at the feet of the Báb.

"Send me not from Thee, O Master," he begged. "Wherever Thou goest, suffer me to follow Thee."

"Muḥammad-'Alí," answered the Báb, "arise, and rest assured that you will be with Me. Tomorrow you shall witness what God has decreed."

Muḥammad-'Alí was the young man who had dreamed that the Báb had come to him and promised that he would die with Him. And now that promise was about to be fulfilled. Two others also rushed up to the Báb, and they were placed in the same cell with Him and Ḥusayn.

That night the Báb's face shone with gladness as He talked to His companions.

The next day, as the Báb was speaking to Ḥusayn, they were interrupted by one of the officers of the barracks who had come to take Ḥusayn away. "Not until I have said to him all those things that I wish to say," the Báb warned the man, "can any earthly power silence Me. Though all the world be armed against Me, yet shall they be powerless to deter Me from fulfilling, to the last word, My intention."

The man was astonished at the Báb's words. He said nothing, however, except to tell Ḥusayn to follow him.

That same morning the young man, Muḥammad-'Alí, was told that if he would turn against the Báb and listen to Him no longer, his life would be spared.

"Never will I renounce my Master" he exclaimed. He is the essence of my faith, and the object of my truest adoration. In Him I have found my paradise. . . ."

So Muḥammad-'Alí was delivered into the hands of Sám Khán, who had charge of the regiment that was to fire upon the Báb. He, too, was to die unless he did what they demanded.

Now Sám Khán was finding it harder and harder to carry out his orders as he came to know his Prisoner. He told the Báb that he was a Christian and did not wish the Báb any wrong. He asked to be freed from having to end His life.

"Follow your instructions," the Báb said, "and if your intention be sincere, the Almighty is surely able to relieve you from your perplexity."

A nail was driven into the wall of the barracks. From this nail the Báb and His companion were to be suspended. Muḥammad-'Alí asked that he be placed so that his body would shield the Báb's. He was suspended in such a way that his head rested on the breast of the Báb.

Seven hundred and fifty soldiers were lined up, and they fired upon the Báb and Muḥammad-'Alí. The smoke of their rifles shut out the light of the sun and turned daylight into darkness.

Many people crowded the tops of the buildings to watch. When the cloud of smoke cleared away, they could hardly believe their eyes. Muḥammad-'Alí stood before them, alive and not in the least hurt. The cord by which the two had been suspended was cut, and the Báb was nowhere in sight.

The soldiers hunted about for Him wildly. They found Him at last in the room where He had spent the night. He was finishing His talk with Ḥusayn—the talk that had been interrupted that morning. Like Muḥammad-'Alí, the Báb was unhurt.

"I have finished My conversation with Siyyid Ḥusayn," He said to the soldier. "Now you may proceed to fulfill your intention."

But Sám Khán was so stunned by what had happened that he ordered his men to leave the barracks at once. He said he would have nothing more to do with killing the Báb, even if it cost him his own life.

Another regiment was brought in. The Báb and His companion were again suspended, and this time the evil command was carried out. The Báb and Muḥammad-'Alí were both killed.

At the very moment the shots were fired a great storm broke over the city. A whirlwind of dust shut out the light of the sun and blinded the eyes of the people who were watching. The entire city remained in darkness from noon until night. But even after all of this had happened, the people still did not realize what a terrible thing they had done.

The wickedness of these people brought great trouble to their country. Many who had watched and had not tried to save the Báb died soon afterward or lost their money and everything they owned. Strange sicknesses that no one knew anything about caused many to die.

As for the second regiment that had fired upon the Báb, they, too, were made to suffer. Some were killed in an earthquake. Others, while resting in the shade of a wall, were killed when the wall fell. The rest were shot because of something they had done.

Now, with the death of the Báb, His enemies felt sure that His Cause would die. But they were very mistaken. Nothing could kill the Cause for which the Báb had died, because that was not God's wish.

Ḥujjat

This is the story of another brave man who was willing to die, if necessary, for the Báb and His Cause. This man lived in Zanján, and his name was Ḥujjat. He was a very wise man, and the people loved him so much that they flocked about him to hear him speak.

When Ḥujjat heard about the Báb and began to give this Message to the people, the religious leaders at once rose up against him. It is strange that they always did this wherever the truth was told.

When Ḥujjat heard about the siege of Shaykh Ṭabarsí, he longed to go and help the brave men in the fort. At that time, however, he was a prisoner in Ṭihrán and could not go. A short time later he escaped by disguising himself and went back to his home. Men, women, and children came out to meet him and wanted to help him in any way they could.

The people of Zanján were warned that anyone who listened to Ḥujjat would be in danger of losing his life. This did not frighten most of Ḥujjat's friends. But they decided to take refuge in a nearby fort because they knew the governor would soon send his soldiers against them. The women and children were taken into the fort with them.

The same thing happened in Zanján that had happened at Shaykh Ṭabarsí and Nayríz. Whenever the governor's army would attack the fort, a few of those within it would rush forth shouting, "O Lord of the Age!" So fierce did they sound that the enemy would scatter before them. Even the people in the town trembled with fright at their cry, which sounded to them almost like thunder. Like other followers of the Báb, however, they would only kill to save the lives of themselves and their women and children.

Trouble came to the fort, however, for they soon ran out of food. All they could get came from a few women who were able to reach the fort. And they had to pay a great deal of money for it.

At this time a young woman named Zaynab from a village nearby wished to help them. She disguised herself as a man and, taking a gun, a sword, and a shield, rushed forth to fight with the other soldiers. No one knew she was a woman, and she was so brave that she made the others feel more courageous. Again they drove back the great force that had come against them.

Ḥujjat, who was watching from the fort, eventually recognized Zaynab and sent out for her to come back. She burst into tears and begged him to tell no one that she was not a man and to let her go back to help her companions. Finally, he let her go.

For five months she fought with the others and encouraged them. She even slept with her head on her sword. She wanted most of all to die for the Cause. And at last one day Zaynab had her wish, for she was shot while helping to drive back the enemy. After her death twenty women became followers of the Báb because of her.

Once Ḥujjat wrote to the Sháh for help, but the letter never reached him. The messenger was captured and put to death. The message from Ḥujjat was destroyed, and another was sent to the Sháh, telling many falsehoods about the brave people in the fort.

The women in the fort helped by baking bread, taking care of the wounded, and cheering and encouraging the soldiers. Even the children were eager to help.

The governor tried to trick them in the same way that those in the other forts had been tricked. Ḥujjat sent a few people to meet with him, but they were either killed or taken prisoner. Only one, a child of nine years, escaped and reached the fort again to tell what had happened.

One day Ḥujjat was struck in the arm by a bullet. Seeing the blood on their beloved leader, the others laid down their guns and rushed to him. It was then that the enemy soldiers were able to enter the fort. A hundred women and children were captured, and later many of them died from the cold.

The men who were not taken prisoner still fought bravely, but every day many were killed. And at last one day, while he was praying to the Báb, Ḥujjat died from the wound he had received in his arm.

Again the enemy thought they had destroyed the Cause of God. But many more people came to believe in the Báb and His Cause because of those who had died so bravely.

Bahá'u'lláh

After the death of the Báb and so many of His brave followers, the government leaders and their friends believed that they would have no more trouble with the Bábís. They were called Bábís because they were followers of the Báb. They were scattered all over the country and were feeling very sad and discouraged because of the terrible things that had happened.

But though one great leader had been taken away, another was to come. The Báb had been telling His followers that He had come to prepare the way for the next divine Teacher Whom God was sending. The Báb called Him "His Holiness" and "Him Whom God shall make manifest."

It was very necessary to prepare the way because at first people are never ready for such a great change. They want to keep the old ways that they have always known. That is the reason so many of them did not want to listen to the Báb. They thought that Muḥammad and the Qur'án were enough for them. But by the time the Message about one new Teacher had been spread all over the country, the path of the second was made easier. Then it was possible to send His Message over the whole world.

So, after the Báb had been martyred, His followers were not alone. His Holiness, Bahá'u'lláh, now gathered them together as much as He could and gave them courage to carry on the teachings of the New Day.

Sometimes people can be very foolish. They do things without stopping to think about what will happen afterward. That was the trouble with two young men who lived in Bahá'u'lláh's country. They tried to kill the Sháh because so many of their Bábí friends had been put to death. They did not succeed, but because of their foolish act, terrible things followed.

Because these young men were Bábís, all of the Bábís were blamed. The people of Persia were very agitated, and many who had nothing to do with what had happened were made to suffer. Even Bahá'u'lláh was blamed because He was now the leader of the Bábís. He was treated with the greatest cruelty and was imprisoned in a dark underground dungeon. His neck and feet were bound with terribly heavy chains. For three days He was given neither food nor drink.

At that time the Most Great Branch was a little boy, eight years old. The Most Great Branch was 'Abdu'l-Bahá, the eldest Son of His Holiness, Bahá'u'lláh. He and the rest of the family were living with an uncle while Bahá'u'lláh was in prison.

Whenever 'Abdu'l-Bahá was sent out on the street, other boys of His age would run after Him, pelting Him with stones. One day He was coming home from the market alone when He looked back and saw a crowd of boys running toward Him with sticks and stones. The only way He could save Himself was to show them that He was not afraid. He went toward them with such a brave and determined air that they turned and ran. After that they never bothered Him again.

When Bahá'u'lláh was put in prison, many of His followers were taken too. Yet in spite of the way they suffered from the terrible place they were in, they were very joyous because Bahá'u'lláh was with them. They even sang there in the darkness. Many of them died, but Bahá'u'lláh was eventually freed. This happened because one of the young men who tried to kill the Sháh confessed that he had done it. All through His life, however, Bahá'u'lláh carried the marks of that terrible prison on His body.

The punishment of the Bábís was now stopped by an order from the Sháh. But as soon as Bahá'u'lláh was released from prison, He was handed another order from the Sháh, saying that He and His family must leave Persia at once. A Russian officer who was in Ṭihrán invited Bahá'u'lláh to go to Russia, where He could live in safety, but Bahá'u'lláh refused, for that was not

God's wish. And so one day, with one of the <u>Sh</u>áh's bodyguards and a Russian officer, Bahá'u'lláh and His family left the country where They had always lived and set out for 'Iráq, over the mountains.

God's Cause Today

When we think back over all the terrible things that happened after Shaykh Aḥmad began to tell people about the Promised One, we may wonder how God's Cause could have survived for us to hear of it today.

In some parts of the world people had learned only about Jesus. In other parts they had learned about Muḥammad, and in others about Moses. Today, because of all the courageous men and women who gave their lives to tell others about the new Teachers, people all over the world know of the Báb and Bahá'u'lláh. Suppose we think about these brave martyrs once more.

Do you remember Shaykh Aḥmad, who was the first to know that it was time for the Promised One to come? Then there was his friend Siyyid Káẓim. Do you remember how he saw the Báb and was invited to His home? Both of these great men told many people about the Báb. It was as if they plowed the ground so that the Cause of God could begin to grow.

After Shaykh Aḥmad and Siyyid Káẓim died, Quddús and Mullá Ḥusayn carried on their work. But do you remember what terrible things happened at Shaykh Ṭabarsí, and how Quddús and Mullá Ḥusayn both gave their lives for God's Cause?

Then there were Vaḥíd and Ḥujjat, who were forced to fight very hard just to live long enough to tell the story of the Promised One. They, too, eventually became martyrs.

Even the Báb, Himself, was killed by the cruel leaders who would not listen to His Message. When He died, His enemies thought that surely they would never hear of that Message again. But that was not what happened.

Bahá'u'lláh was left, and all of those who had heard and believed the Báb's Message turned to Him. But then another very tragic thing happened. Two young men who called themselves Bábís but did not understand the Báb's teachings tried to kill the Sháh. As a result, all of the Bábís were blamed, even Bahá'u'lláh.

Ṭáhirih, the brave woman who helped Persian women so much, and who taught about the Promised One, was put to death. All the Letters of the Living were either killed or put in prison or sent out of the country. And many, many others died, even women and children.

As if that were not enough, Bahá'u'lláh was banished, or sent away from the country where He had been born and had always lived. He and His family had to cross the mountains in the bitter cold of winter and make their home in a country called 'Iráq. From there they went to Palestine, which is the Holy Land because so many of the divine Teachers have lived there.

It is no wonder that the Sháh believed he would never hear about the Báb or Bahá'u'lláh or Their Message again. But how mistaken he was and how foolish! There is something in this great Cause of God that would not let it be killed.

It is said that the very darkest time of night is just before dawn. That is the way it was with God's Cause. Its enemies believed that it had entirely disappeared and that they would never hear of it again. But that was just the time when it began to grow stronger and stronger.

The Sháh did not know it because he thought he was so great and powerful, but he was only a tool that God had used to carry the Cause to another country. In that country Bahá'u'lláh was given much more freedom to spread His Message. Today it has spread all over the world. Those who are a part of it are no longer called Bábís. They are called Bahá'ís, which means "followers of Bahá'u'lláh." There are Bahá'ís in every country in the world, and books of the Báb, Bahá'-u'lláh, and 'Abdu'l-Bahá are printed in over eight hundred languages so that people everywhere can read them.

The Cause of God is like a tree. At first, when Shaykh Aḥmad started out to teach about the Promised One, it was like planting a little seed. This seed has grown and grown until now many people throughout the world are sheltered beneath its branches.

'Abdu'l-Bahá brought the great news about the Báb and Bahá'u'lláh to America, to England, and to many other countries. Do you remember the story of 'Abdu'l-Bahá when He was a young boy and the other children were unkind to Him? That was while His Father, Bahá'u'lláh, was in prison.

Now Bahá'u'lláh and 'Abdu'l-Bahá have both gone on to that beautiful kingdom to which we shall go when our work in this world is done. But all the time the Cause of God is growing. Someday everyone in the whole world will know about it, because those who do know about it are happiest when they are telling someone else about it.

Perhaps someday you will be one of those teachers who travels to faraway places and tells people about Bahá'u'lláh and the New Day. We do not know yet what great things these teachers will do. At the time when the Báb and Bahá'u'lláh lived, there was much fighting and killing, but in the New Day, which is just beginning now, Bahá'u'lláh tells us there will be no more wars.

Won't it be a beautiful world when everyone is kind and thoughtful of others and will never want to hurt anyone? We can begin that right now, just as the Báb began when He was very young. Then God will help us just as He helped those who first left their homes to tell others of the Promised One.

Glossary of Symbols

The majority of symbols appearing in the illustrations of *Children's Stories from the Dawn-Breakers* are taken from the designs of Oriental carpets. The explanation for each symbol is based on information from the following sources:

Blair, Sheila S., and Jonathan M. Bloom. *The Art and Architecture of Islam 1250–1800*. Yale University Press Pelican History of Art. New Haven, Conn.: Yale University Press, 1994.

Meyer, Franz Sales. *Handbook of Ornament: A Grammar of Art, Industrial and Architectural Designing in All Its Branches for Practical As Well As Theoretical Use*. New York: Dover Publications, 1957.

Thompson, Jon. *Oriental Carpets: From the Tents, Cottages and Workshops of Asia*. N.p.: E. P. Dutton, 1993.

Train, John. *Oriental Rug Symbols: The Figure in the Carpet*. London: Philip Wilson Publishers Limited, 1997.

Ware, Joyce C. *The Official Price Guide to Oriental Rugs*. New York: House of Collectibles, 1996.

The symbols have been adapted to enhance the visual impact of the illustrations and should not be taken as literal interpretations of the text. Historically, in some cases, there may be two or even three other meanings associated with a single symbol in addition to the explanation given here. In other cases the illustrator has created more contemporary symbols based on the historic meaning. These are designated by an asterisk.*

The cultures that gave rise to the symbols include those of Arabia, China, Chinese Turkestan, Egypt, Indochina, Mongolia, Persia, Turkmenistan, and various nomadic peoples of the East. Many of the symbols are also associated with various religions including Hinduism, Buddhism, Zoroastrianism, Judaism, Christianity, Islam, the Bábí Faith, and the Bahá'í Faith.

Animals, Birds, Fish:

Dove or White Bird: Faith, offering peace.*

Eagle: Nobility, dignity, integrity.*

Fish: Implies liberation and struggling against difficulties; may also suggest love.*

Horse: Nobility, strength.*

Lion: Bravery, strength.*

Nightingale: Associated with Bahá'u'lláh.*

Borders:

Running Dog Border: Sometimes used to indicate fear.

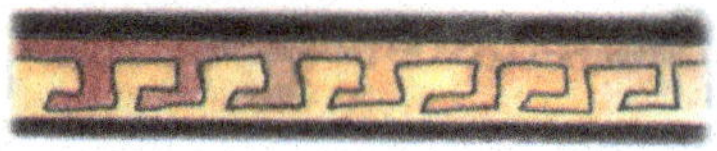

Running Water: The symbol of running water meant eternity to the Egyptians.

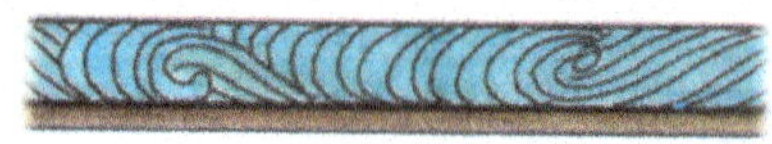

The letter "S": On old Persian carpets this symbolizes light and godliness; when it appears in the shape of a serpent it represents human wisdom.

Checker Pattern: A stylized symbol of the sun, representing light, knowledge.

Clouds, Cloud Bands, or Chi:

Clouds (stylized): A symbol of purity.*

Cloud Collar: Radiating energy.

Diamonds: A religious symbol in all oriental carpets; signifies creation.

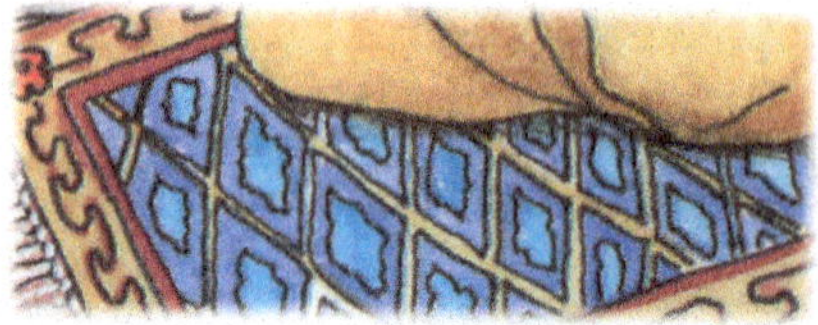

Flowers:

Carnation: From Asia Minor and Morocco—symbolizes prayer.

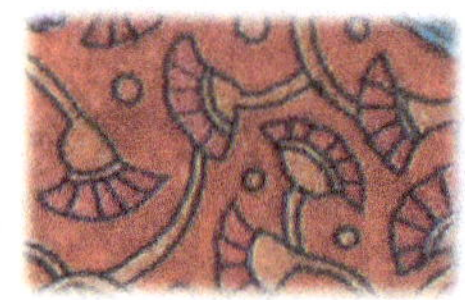

Iris: The tongue shape of the iris gave it the position of interpreter. It was also a symbol of religious freedom and liberation from earthly ties.

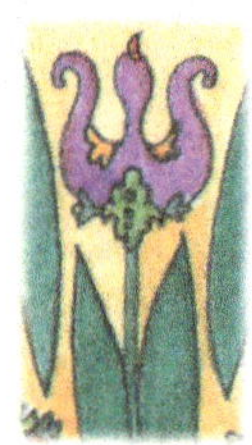

Lily: Purity and spirituality.

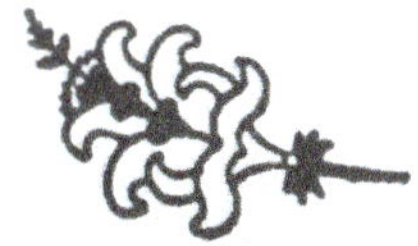

Rinceau or Flower Meander: A universal theme from Europe to China (see explanations of individual flowers and leaves).

Rose or Rosette: In Persia, divine power was ascribed to the rose. It was the symbol of eternal life as well.

Gul: The word means "flower" or "rose" in Persian.

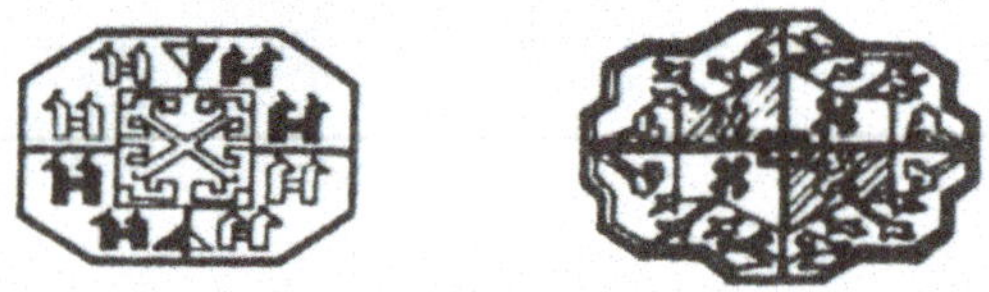

Memling Gul: Hooked or stepped—indicates the gateway to paradise.

Kufesque: Named after the Mesopotamian town of Kufa, this symbol originally may have been Arabic script meaning "God is Great."

LEAVES: Implies endless regeneration and thus immortality.

MOUNTAINS: The Mongols believed that the souls of just men flew from the mountain peaks to heaven; also indicates the center of the universe, rising from the soul of eternity.

NINE-POINTED STAR: A symbol associated with the Bahá'í Faith, thereby representing unity, equality, elimination of prejudice.*

Paisley or Boteh: Can mean the soul and immortality, although in this book it is also used simply as a decorative motif on clothing.

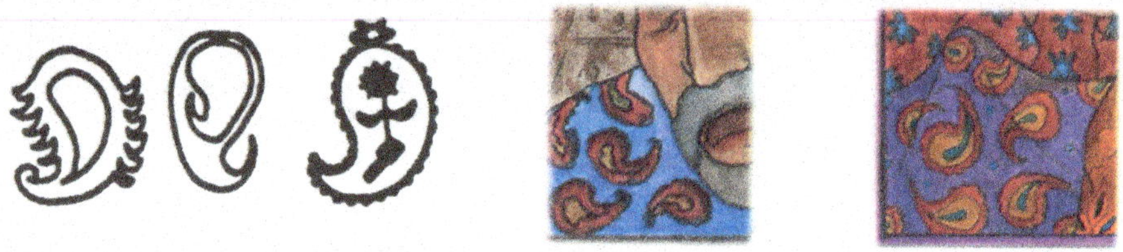

Sun: Light, knowledge, divine guidance.*

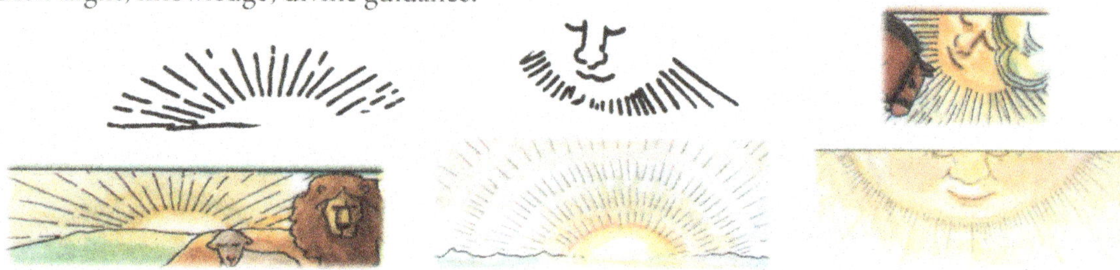

Tendrils and Stems: Endurance, repetition, eternity.

Trees:

Tree of Life: One of the oldest and most universal symbols of humankind; a reminder of the passage from this existence into a higher life.

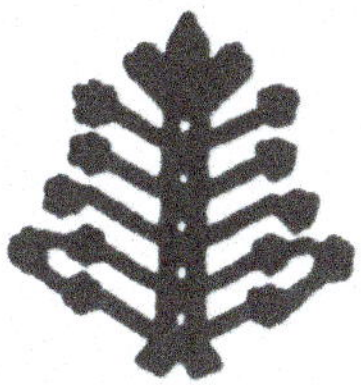

Weeping Willow: Usually found in funerary carpets.

Waves and Foam: In Chinese Turkestan, believed to suggest philosophy, overcoming adversity.*